FOUND

Memoirs of a Mountain Missionary

Allen and Jennie Britt

ACKNOWLEDGMENTS

In addition to the loved ones who have shared their memories, I would like to acknowledge my debt of gratitude to the following:

Brother Brian Wagner, my colleague at Virginia Baptist College, who graciously volunteered his time to edit the manuscript. It was a joy to work with you, Brother!

Brother Todd LeFort, who offered to guide me through the publishing process. You were an answer to prayer, Brother!

And to Gary and Becky Noakes, cherished friends who provided the computer equipment to make this and future projects possible.

DEDICATION

To the only wise God our Saviour

My Strength in weakness,

My Wisdom in perplexity,

My Help in distress,

My Comfort in sorrow,

My Companion in loneliness,

My Counselor-King

be glory and majesty, dominion and power, both

now and ever. Amen

Jude 25

TABLE OF CONTENTS

Introduction

Chapter

INTRODUCTION

A tall, lanky teenager roamed the woods of the family farm on the Yellow River in Gwinnett County, Georgia. He had much on which to ruminate: the family poverty, for one topic. How would he provide for himself when he stepped over the threshold of his teen years into adulthood? Farming? Even for his dad, farming did not adequately provide for his family. Continue working in a store? Wasn't there anything more meaningful for him to devote his life?

What was his purpose in life? What was he meant to do? Was there anything to give significance to an otherwise insignificant existence? Would he always be a nobody, wondering why he was here?

Older brothers Greg and Tom seemed to have earned recognition for themselves. Greg, even before he embarked on a military career, had earned recognition as a star athlete in his local high school. Tom, long before he rose to prominence in the music world, was already a recognized scholar. He could succeed in any direction he chose to travel.

What was there for him? He could see no outstanding qualities in his own life that would lead to a significant, or even a meaningful, existence.

Unknown to this teenager, while he was seeking direction and meaning for his life, One was seeking him— One whose purposes would give direction and meaning to his own life, One whose plan would give him significance, a significance reaching far beyond this life and into eternity. Here is his story—the story of one "found in him," recorded in the Monday afternoons of his retirement up to the time of his first stroke, September 10, 2010. (His mornings were committed to a Bible study at a local assisted-living facility. I was working Tuesday through Friday at the Virginia Baptist College/ Faith Baptist School Library.)

Since Allen's passing to Heaven—February 10, 2014—family members and friends have graciously added their memories to our own. Chapter 1 features many of their memories. Thanks to all of you! Chapters titled "Meanwhile" and the afterword are my own. And research has supplied details not available otherwise.

Our prayer is that this record will encourage the next generation to walk with God and seek His direction and blessing.

"One generation shall praise thy works to another, and shall declare thy mighty acts." Psalm 145:4

Jennie Britt

Chapter 1

SPARED

Fire! Fire! Fire! Flames leaped to the skies. One woman scurried to rescue pre-schoolers from the blazing house.

With a wood-burning stove in the living room to heat the house and a wood-burning cook stove in the kitchen, it was easy for a wood frame house to catch fire. In December of 1942, the Britt family home caught fire and burned to the ground. Although there were three pre-schoolers in the family at the time, only two were at home: Doris, born March 5th of that year, and Hellen, born May 17, 1939. Allen, Hellen's fraternal twin, was at Scottish Rite Hospital. Tom, only five, had already been taught to read by his father; he had been put on the school bus and sent to school. Mom Britt reportedly said, "If I'd had one more child to get out of that house, I wouldn't have made it!"

Tom remembers, "Annie met us at the bus to tell us that the house had burned. When we got home we saw only ashes and chimneys where the house had been."

Greg remembers being told at school that the house was on fire. He remembers the overwhelming feeling of helplessness. The fortress of his first seven years survived only in his memory: the wide, welcoming front porch with its swing and chairs; the coat rack standing guard in the front hall; the living room with its fabric couch, its wind-up record player, its pump organ, its battery-operated radio (for company only), its commanding mantle; the bedrooms with their beds & dressers; the kitchen with its room-length table and china cabinet; the back porch with its view of the huge cottonwood tree and the walnut trees beyond. All gone! Even the smoke house with its precious store of meat had burned to the ground.

After the fire the family moved one mile away to a rental house on Bethesda Church Road across from Bethesda School. Neighbors and church families donated clothes. The WPA donated clothes.

"Daddy got a job with the shoe factory in Lawrenceville," Greg recalled. "Before that, he was farming: growing cotton; raising hogs to butcher, cows to milk, mules to plow; churning milk to make butter; taking milk and butter to the spring to get cold.

The spring was also the source of drinking water. (Water from the well had the taste of lime.) The spring was the site for washing clothes with its big black wash-pot. And the spring was also the site for hog-killing. The hogs would be hung in the trees and water boiled in the wash-pot.

At the time of the fire, Aunt Annie was still working at the canning plant in Snellville. Later, there was an explosion at the plant and the other three people who worked there were all killed. After the fire and the family's move to Bethesda, Aunt Annie worked in the school cafeteria." Allen remembered walking to school with Aunt Annie.

Allen had been spared the experience of the family fire by being hospitalized when it happened. He was spared a second life-threatening experience after the family moved to Bethesda. He remembered:

"When we lived in Bethesda we walked to school. One day Aunt Annie and I were walking to –or from—school. We got to the intersection of Bethesda Road and Route 29. I walked into the road right in front of a gas truck. Aunt Annie grabbed me and pulled me out of the road. She yanked me out of that road and saved my life."

Allen remembered on another occasion being spared a life-threatening encounter with a snake. He and his brother Tom were walking toward the spring when Tom warned him that he saw a snake ahead. Allen heard the warning and moved quickly to avoid the encounter.

From the time of his birth—May 17, 1939, through his growing-up years, it seemed apparent to all who knew him that Allen had been spared for a purpose, that God had planned for him a unique place of service. One sister said of Allen during those years, "He was my only older brother who was kind to his little sisters. He was my only brother who showed compassion . . . to my mother." Not just the events from which his life had been spared, but the circumstances, the people, the events that shaped his life— all were a part of God's plan.

Here is his story as he tells it.

Chapter 2

SCHOOL DAYS

The playground at Bethesda School where I attended school from 1st through 11th grade was a hub of activity. Girls were jumping rope. Boys were playing marbles in the sand. Fights were common.

I remember once saying to an opponent, "I'm going to get my sister and she's going to beat you up." When I found her, she was fighting someone else on the other side of the playground. She'd fight at the drop of a hat, and she'd even drop the hat!

Sympathy wasn't wasted on minor injuries. Once I was playing with my cousin Daryl. We were climbing on cement blocks and I fell and hurt my back. "Oh, my back is broken," I moaned. "Your back's not broken," Daryl returned. "You wouldn't be able to move if your back were broken."

Among the teachers who influenced those years, some were stellar. The 2nd grade teacher, tall, middle-aged Miss Hamilton, told stories: "The Bremen Town Musicians," "The Billy Goats Gruff." The stories came alive. She was a master storyteller. She instilled a love of stories that never left me.

The 6th grade teacher, Miss Lula Brown, was a legend. She drove an old Chevrolet Coupe. She never got it out of 2nd gear. She'd always have a line of cars behind her.

She was so tiny, but she feared no one. She kept a 6-foot hickory switch in her broom closet. We heard the stories, but our class never saw her switch. The legend was enough to keep us in line! I had had enough hickory switches at home to know I didn't want to meet Miss Lula Brown's.

In 7th grade I sat in the back of the room. I had made a facial mask and was attracting attention with it. The teacher, J. Troy Buice, saw me and told me to come to the front of the room and show the class. I was too embarrassed, so I didn't. So he invited me to come see him at recess. I went to see him and he stretched me across his desk and paddled me. I gave up my theatrical career on the spot.

At the end of the school year, J. Troy Buice took the class to Calloway Gardens as an end-of-school activity. He also took his grandson, 2 or 3 years younger. Several students wrestled Mr. Buice to toss him into a stream. The grandson tackled two students who had Mr. Buice locked in a bear hug and tumbled them all in the stream!

In 8th grade, two other guys and I cheated on a civics test. The teacher sent us to the principal, and he paddled us. That ended my career of banditry!

In 9th grade we had an initiation into the Future Farmers of America. We had to memorize the Farmer's Creed: "I believe in the future of farming . . . ." Older students listened to us recite the Farmer's Creed. I had heard rumors about the initiation--those who couldn't recite it were blindfolded and thrown from the stage floor to the gym floor and caught in a sheet. One boy had to eat a peanut butter pie. He got half of it down when it came back up! -- so I learned that Farmer's Creed!

Agriculture class made sweet potato crates to be sold to farmers. The class also planted pine trees in Gwinnett County. They were 5"-6" seedlings of loblolly pine.

Everyone had to have a farm project. My project was the family cow. I fed her, milked her, and kept a record of how much milk she gave. I also kept records of field work, such as cutting brush.

After we moved to Brookhaven in 1955, I enrolled in Latin class. It was the first class of the day. Mrs. Tribble, an older woman, was the Latin teacher. Every day we'd recite

the pledge of allegiance and the Lord's Prayer. We learned

vocabulary. We did conjugations and declensions. At the

end of the year we had a Roman banquet. Everyone dressed

in costumes. The students who made better grades (A's and

B's) were patricians. The students who made lower grades

(C's and D's) were plebians. Plebians served patricians.

John Brenner and I were asked to serve drinks. We bought a

lemon drink and served it.

After I had been saved, our Bible club from school

went to a Baptist church. The preacher asked, "Do any of

you know the Lord?" I raised my hand. He quizzed me in a

mocking tone: "How do you know the Lord? Have you met

him? Were you introduced to him?" He was evidently a

liberal who didn't believe in personal salvation.

Chapter 3

MEANWHILE

Meanwhile, 270 miles away, another student entered school at Liberty Homes Elementary School in North Charleston, South Carolina. Although it was to become a love affair with learning, her education did not begin that way. It began with many tears and strong crying.

"Lillian," she sobbed to the first-grade classmate known to her from her church, "tell the teacher we want to go home." "No, Jennie, you tell her," was the tearful reply.

By second grade, the tears had been abandoned for a wholehearted involvement in the school experience. Recess offered the exhilarating opportunity to participate in the favorite sport of chasing boys. Under the spreading live oaks, boys and girls would dodge and dart until someone was tagged and dragged to the tree that had been designated as prison. One runner would stand guard lest someone not yet tagged should touch and free the prisoner. When that happened, the chase was on again!

Two teachers from elementary years must have seen the budding promise of a future teacher and offered this student an opportunity to teach. The third grade teacher was the first to present this opportunity when she offered her the chance of calling out spelling words for a spelling bee.

All went well until she came to L. H., the neighbor boy with whom she had been riding bicycles. "L. H., . . . honey," she solemnly called, and the class howled in laughter.

The fifth grade teacher offered the second opportunity to teach—this time a lesson on the three branches of government. Whether or not the students remembered the lesson, that fifth-grade "teacher" remembered it well as her first taste of the joys of teaching.

Sixth grade opened the door for this student to a lifelong love affair with history. Whether ancient history or modern, whether American history or world history, each lesson opened the door to an adventure. Each teacher pulled back the curtain on a real-life drama.

Music already played a major role in this student's life: The Firestone Hour, the Metropolitan Opera on the radio; Marian Anderson, Glenn Gould, other artists on recordings. Sixth grade marked the beginning of private lessons on piano, a pursuit that was to continue through 11th grade in high school and through her 4th year of college. Soon after beginning piano, came the experience that was to elevate this student's love of music to a new level: the annual Charleston Choral Society production of The Messiah. Here was music that lifted the soul to the very gates of Heaven! She would be music's devotee forever after.

In her junior year in high school this student's pastor recommended her for a position as pianist of a mission church started by her home church. There, she also became a Sunday School teacher—her first experience in missionary church planting!

Chapter 4

HOME SWEET HOME
(Allen's story continued)

My earliest memories are of coming home from school and changing clothes from school clothes, which we wore all week, to play clothes, which were older clothes. I remember coming home to Mother's snacks: homemade tea cakes (cookies) or biscuits. If there were biscuits, we'd open them up, butter them, melt the butter, and sprinkle sugar on top. If there were left-over cornbread, we'd crumble it up in sweet milk or buttermilk from our own cow.

After snacks I'd go out and make myself a toy: airplanes out of wood scraps (I flew lots of planes that way.), boats out of pine bark (I'd launch them in the sand.), toy pistols out of wood (I'd hunt for birds, tigers, lions.). Or, I'd work on my farm project for agriculture class. I fed and milked the family cow twice a day and recorded what I fed her, how much I fed her, and how much milk she gave. At first, I got a quart of milk; later, a half gallon. I also recorded how much time I spent cutting brush. As an early teen (twelve or thirteen) I inherited the job of building the fire in the stove as well as milking the cow.

We were glad to see Dad come in from work, because then we could eat. Supper would be beans and cornbread, greens in season, once in a while pork chops. (We killed a hog every year. We cured the meat: rubbed it with a salt/sugar combination. We processed ham, bacon, sausage.) After supper we'd scatter to do homework.

Mom did everything herself—cooking, cleaning house, laundry. She'd scrub the clothes on a scrub board, then rinse in a second tub, then wring them out and hang them on the line.

She cooked dried beans, biscuits, corn bread. On Sunday we had green beans, mashed potatoes, fried chicken, biscuits and gravy. (Aunt Annie had killed and plucked the chicken.) After we had eaten the last crumb, she brought out a beautiful coconut cake. Dad had bought the coconut, and Mother had grated it. The eggs had been separated, and Mother had beaten the whites to a foamy froth.

On Sunday morning we would all get in the road and walk to church, except Mother. She'd stay home and cook Sunday dinner for 15 people—the eleven of us, and always company—relatives.

One of those Sunday visitors was Grandpa Davis, the only living grandparent. Pa Davis had attended Cornell University and studied to be a preacher. The war intervened in his studies. During the war, he trained to be an intelligence photographer. Later, he had a photography studio in Tuscaloosa, Alabama. His second wife (Grandma Davis had died) was a beautician. She had a beauty parlor in the other end of his studio.

Not only did Grandpa Davis come for Sunday visits, he came also for photography sessions. Once when I was 9 or 10, he took me to the fair. He gave me $4.00 to spend, and I spent it all in 10 minutes. I bought cotton candy. It made my teeth hurt, then it was gone. It evaporated in my mouth like the $4.00 evaporated in my hand.

After church, we'd come in and change clothes. We'd eat in shifts—the grown-ups first, then the children. We'd sit around and talk or listen to the grown-ups tell their stories. If we didn't have company, Daddy would pile everybody in the car and we'd all go for a ride. One place we'd go was Stone Mountain—15 or 20 miles from us.

Recreation for us children would be baseball. Someone would make a bat out of wood. We'd roll a couple of socks together and tape the roll to make a baseball. When someone hit the ball, it would fly apart. We'd tape it back together and keep on playing.

In summer, we'd swim together in the Yellow River in old clothes. The Yellow River flowed through our pasture. It was our own swimming hole. The older children would threaten, "You can jump in, or we'll throw you in." I'd jump in.

Summer recreation also included reading. I remember walking to Gloster and getting books to read from the bookmobile. One summer I got a certificate for reading 26 books.

An aunt would give me comic books to read. She'd say, "Don't let them get torn up." But they would be torn up by family members who would roll them up and use them as weapons.

Mom would usually defer discipline to Dad. She would say if we were bad, "I'll tell your Dad when he comes home." He never said, "Go to your room," because no one had his own room. All the girls slept in one room, and all the boys slept in one room.

From the beginning, I experienced a rocky relationship with the women in my life: five sisters! I'd aggravate my sisters until they beat on me. Then I'd go for a long walk to recuperate from my hurt feelings. I'd explore the woods and follow the trails to see where they went. After a while, I'd say, "Now, where am I?" Then I'd try to find the river and follow the river to the road and take the river road home. I'd be thinking about how to solve the world's problems: how to have a truce with my combatant sisters.

Television introduced a new form of entertainment to the community. Occasionally I'd go to a relative's house to watch baseball on TV. I remember the commercial, "Carpets from the looms of Mohawk."

At home Dad was known to be subject to bouts of anger. One night there was a flare-up and Dad picked up a chair and threw it at the wall. It bounced off the wall and hit him on the head. All the anger suddenly drained away.

In the community, Dad was known as the song leader of the local Baptist church. On one occasion our church was having a revival meeting. I went over early because I knew my dad was coming to the meeting. Someone said, "Here he comes!" I took off running to meet him so I could sit with my dad. He was leading the singing.

But Dad could be an effective teacher as well. When I was still a student at Bethesda I found a $1 bill on the steps of the school and picked it up and put it in my pocket. I stopped at the store on the way home and spent a nickel or a dime. The change was jingling in my pocket when I got home, and my father heard it. He asked me where I got the money, and I told him. He said, "Give me the change, and I'll give you a $1 bill so that you can take it back to the school office." I learned to return and not to claim things I found that didn't belong to me.

In March of my early days as a Future Farmer I decided I would plant a garden. I got the hoe out and started hoeing a broom sage patch. I decided that was hard work. So, I thought, "Why not strike a match and burn off the broom sage?"

So I got a match and set fire to the broom sage.
Then the wind took over and blew it all over the field. I was
running around trying to put it out, but it was running wild.
It blew from the field to the woods. By then other people
were aware of the fire. It burned most of our 200 acres
before it started burning other people's property.

Mrs. Baucom, who lived a mile away, said she "fit fire
till midnight."

Daddy came home about dark. By then the fire had
burned most of the property.

"Who started this fire?" he demanded. When I was
named as the culprit, he took his belt off and administered a
sound whipping. There were two sounds: the sound of the
belt lashing my legs and the sound of my hollering and
screaming and jumping.

He took me to the back porch and said, "Look what
you've done!"

That whipping changed my life. It made me more conscientious. It made me more careful. It made me more considerate of property and of the consequences of my actions.

But there was another disciplinarian and another powerful influence in my life. Our family lived with my dad's older sister Aunt Annie. Aunt Annie had inherited the family farm from her parents, Grandma and Grandpa Britt. (Their house had burned earlier.) She built the home place on the land.

Aunt Annie not only provided a home for us, she also took it on herself to correct the children. When discipline was needed, she'd make you go get a hickory switch and, if it wasn't big enough, she'd make you go back and get another one. The boys were made to roll up their pants legs and get switched on their bare legs.

The more I think about the influence of Aunt Annie on my life, the more I realize she shaped my character. She tried to see to it that I was an early riser. She would awaken me out of a sound sleep to go to the barn and be her bodyguard while she milked the cow. I would lean against the wall and go back to sleep. Then I would be awakened by a feeling of warm liquid splashing over me. Aunt Annie would be spraying me with milk from the cow's udder.

One morning Aunt Annie called me to get up, and I got up and sat on the side of the bed and went back to sleep. She came back and saw me sleeping and slapped my face. I saw stars for two weeks!

But we knew Aunt Annie cared for us. Once when we were living at Bethesda, Aunt Annie was at home on a cold, icy day. She was wearing a gray sweater. When we came in, she told us not to put our hand by the stove (a big, round, coal-burning stove). She knew that, if you have very cold hands and you put them near a stove, it will cause a painful, pricking sensation. Instead, she put them inside her sweater and warmed them with her body heat.

In winter I had to bring in coal –in a coal bucket. I'd take the axe and break up the coal and bring it in in the bucket. A sibling observes, "To know Allen, you must know this drill sergeant-type lady had a lot to do with his determination to learn how to do chores and be manly. . . Allen was taught by said Aunt Annie to milk cows, mend fences, cut firewood, build fires in our wood cook stove as well as our wood heater. . . She would not allow Allen to be less than what he could be with her, (ahem) . . . encouragement!"

Annie was friends with a family in Atlanta. They both got cancer, and she went to take care of them. They both died, and Annie came back to Gloster.

Some time after that, she thought she had cancer. One morning she walked from the home place to the railroad tracks—a mile away, halfway between home and Alford's Store, where I was working. The engineer saw her sitting on the tracks, and blew the horn, but she never moved.

I was working at the store when the train people came to get a tub to put her body in. I remember running home to tell the family. I didn't cry for three days. Then I wept and wept and wept with grief.

Aunt Annie's death devastated my dad. My dad wept and wouldn't eat. Eventually he went to bed with grief and illness. He couldn't work for about 3 months. I thought we were going to starve.

During that time I went to visit Dutton's. David was my age; Lamar was Tom's age. While I was there, their dad gave me vegetables from the garden—tomatoes, corn, beans—to take home.

Another time I walked to Alford's Store in Gloster. While I was there, Pastor Fowler came in. He bought some groceries—flour, beans, etc.—and gave them to me to take home.

Greg sent money home from his Air Force pay. I didn't think Daddy was going to survive. Eventually, he did get well and moved us to Atlanta.

Earlier, Daddy had worked at Rich's Department Store in downtown Atlanta. Then he rode with someone else to work. He drove our car to Uncle Thurman's grocery store on Route 29 where he met his ride. Aunt Essie Mae, Thurman's wife, would dun us for the groceries Daddy charged.

After we moved to Brookhaven, Daddy would ride the bus to Atlanta. He went back to work at Rich's as a shoe salesman. He would take off a customer's shoe, measure the foot, bring them a pair of shoes, and tie them on their feet.

When we needed shoes, he would put our bare foot on a sheet of newspaper, draw around the foot, cut out the drawing, and take it to town to fit it for shoes. (Daddy had started out making shoes at a manufacturer's in Lawrenceville.)

After we moved to Atlanta, when I needed shoes, I'd get on a trolley and ride to town. I'd get off the trolley and walk to Rich's in downtown Atlanta. Daddy would fit me with shoes—leather shoes—and pay for them.

I was not aware of Dad's drinking until after we moved to Atlanta. (I was told that he had had drinking sprees before.) He'd come home drunk. He'd also drink Miles Nervine, a nerve tonic. It poisoned his brain so that he was incoherent for a while. We had to admit him to a hospital to help him overcome his addiction.

Many things were different when we moved to Brookhaven. For one thing, my chores were different. There were no longer cows to milk. Daddy bought me an electric lawn mower. My job was to cut the grass on a ½-acre lot.

For another, summers were different. There was no longer Aunt Annie to awaken me with her rousing words, "An idle mind is the devil's workshop." I'd sleep late. No one would bother me except the flies. They would land on me until I crawled under the sheet. Then I'd get hot and come out to face the flies.

One thing that changed little was the celebration of Christmas. I remember the parties at school in the early days. All the sweets available tempted me to gorge myself. Then I would suffer diarrhea for a couple of days.

At home we'd have a tree—3' to 4'. Someone was always knocking it over—fighting, playing, rough-housing. The day after Christmas Mother would take the decorations off and throw it in the yard. I remember one or two years we had a ceramic tree with lights.

Gifts were clothing, nuts, and fruit—apples and oranges. Apples and oranges were a Christmas treat, not something we had all year. We would hang stockings and the fruit and nuts would be put in the stockings. One year I got a flannel shirt for Christmas. I wore that flannel shirt all winter for a coat.

Chapter 5

MEANWHILE II

Meanwhile, family life for the young lady 270 miles away was developing around four cornerstones: work, recreation, hospitality, and ministry. Work, of course, was the chief cornerstone. Her favorite household chore was washing dishes under the shade of the spreading live oak just outside the kitchen window. In summer the most time-consuming chore was gardening: picking and preparing for canning the mountains of green beans, field peas, and lima beans that her mother canned for the winter store. In other seasons the most time-consuming chore was washing and waxing the family car—with Blondie, the family cocker spaniel, nipping at her heels.

The motivation for the chores—besides the fact that it was expected and one dared not fail to fulfill expectations—was the recreation that awaited when chores were done. On Dad's day off, recreation could be a drive to the ocean for a swim. To be borne up by the unseen power of the waves seemed both a mystery and a miracle. How could the waves that buffeted one about when standing hold one up when one rested on their surface? Maybe swimming was an act of faith. It seemed so to this young swimmer!

On other days—when Dad was working and the chores were done— backyard baseball beckoned. Neighbor boys came from all directions: David Price from one side of the house, David and Jimmy Dill from behind the house, the Goodwin boys from the other side. There was always plenty of action. With no umpire to call balls and strikes, the batter had to either get a hit, pop out, ground out, or go down swinging!

When there were not enough players to make up teams, bicycling offered diversion. This young lady had been taught to ride a bicycle by a cousin who offered to hold the bicycle while she made wobbling efforts to maintain balance. Soon she was keeping balance without the guiding hand. But, alas, she failed to learn the fine art of stopping the bicycle before she made her first excursion to the corner grocery store. On arrival, there was nothing to do but crash into the front of the store to stop the bicycle!

The realm of the imagination offered plenty of entertainment: reading remained a favorite pastime, as did climbing trees. From the top of the favorite tree, one could be a look-out watching for enemy ships or a traveler, watching for first sight of a foreign shore.

The home's hospitality opened a window to the world. Visiting missionaries and evangelists frequently graced the table. A visiting sailor or airman in the Sunday services at church would prompt an impromptu invitation to dinner. Dad did the inviting. Mom prepared the meal. The girls helped: sweetening the tea, making the lemonade,

watching the chicken frying in the huge iron frying pan.

Perhaps the crowning moment of hospitality came

the day Dr. Charles Weigle came as a guest. Here was a

world-renowned evangelist. Here was the hymn-writer of

the much-loved "No One Ever Cared for Me Like Jesus."

Surely, she felt, this was what it meant to "entertain angels

unawares." (Hebrews 13:1)

Hospitality and ministry merged for one set of guests

who came regularly for a Friday night Bible study. Two

young couples from the church, one a pair of locals, the

other an Air Force couple, met with the family for Bible

study, followed by refreshments. The meeting place rotated

from one home to another. Here was on-the-job training for

a young lady, who, as wife of a missionary church planter,

would one day entertain all the visiting evangelists and

missionaries.

But ministry reached out of the home as well. This young lady's first invitation to serve as an accompanist came in the form of an invitation to accompany her dad's Sunday School class for their opening assembly. The class met in one of the rooms of the children's home located across the street from the church.

At age thirteen she had joined her parents in a hospital ministry, visiting from bed to bed in the wards of the Old Roper Hospital. Here, unlimited opportunity awaited: to read God's Word, to pray with the sick and the dying, to point willing sinners to the One who saves those who come unto God by Him. Here, too, was the challenge of allowing the love of God to overcome the natural recoil of the flesh from the repulsive. One patient, evidently suffering an advanced stage of cancer, presented a pitiful sight, with one side of her face literally eaten away. The stench of decaying flesh was overwhelming. Yet, God's grace enabled the mother and daughter to tarry long enough to pray with this one so near to eternity.

If work, recreation, hospitality and ministry were the cornerstones of family life, Mom was the foundation and Dad the architect of family life. Mom was always there—to oversee household chores, to offer after-school treats, whether a pot of black-eyed peas left over from dinner or a pot of boiled peanuts prepared for the occasion. Although assistance may be called for—to hang out clothes, or to iron designated garments, laundry remained her domain, as did meal preparation. Meals relied heavily on produce from the garden—cucumbers, tomatoes, greens in season; green beans, corn, lima beans, field peas year-round, fresh from the garden or from the canned (or frozen) store. Fried fish from fishing expeditions was a staple, as were chicken and rabbit from the chickens and rabbits raised to supply the table. Every meal seemed a feast, but there were special-occasion treats as well, such as homemade ice cream churned on the back steps or Mom's exquisite lemon-sponge pie. Mom's characteristic humming as she worked lit the household with her joy—the joy of serving those she loved.

Dad remained the undisputed head of the household. It was he who assigned chores and it was he who assigned consequences for chores not done. When Dad came home for dinner from his barber shop just 3 blocks away, woe to the delinquent who had not done his assignments! He would be sent to finish the uncompleted work while the rest of the family sat down to eat!

It was also Dad who started the young ones working outside the home. The boys would be taken at an early age to the barber shop to offer shoe-shining services to the customers there. Sometimes they would offer boiled peanuts for sale to nearby businesses.

This daughter, when she was in high school and exempt from exams, thought it a treat to be taken with Dad on his milk route. The quiet of the early rising, 4:00 A. M.,

was followed by the delight of breakfast with Dad; then, the

excitement of loading at the dairy: crates of milk sliding

noisily about; finally, blocks of ice sliding down the ramp at

the ice house. Dad chipped the blocks into smaller slivers to

keep the milk cold until delivered and to keep the milkman's

helper cool as the morning progressed.

Dad was also the architect of family outings: fishing,

swimming, flower shows, chamber music at the Gibbs Art

Gallery. Family vacations, too, were his plan—usually

camping in the mountains of South Carolina. The milk truck

provided accommodations for the first of these camping

vacations. Cots were hung from rods at either end of the

truck bed: Mom and Dad on the upper bunks, sisters on the

lower bunks, so close that when one turned on her side, she

was touching the bunk above. The boys slept on a mattress

on the bed of the truck—close fellowship for a family of

seven! The mountain vacations—usually at Table Rock State

Park or Oconee State Park—offered swimming, rowing, hiking the mountain trails as well as cooking and eating in the great outdoors. After the first camping vacation, accommodations upgraded to tents!

In spite of the busyness of working two jobs—the milk route and the barber shop—and the effort of raising a large garden, Dad found time for an absorbing avocation— raising camellias. His camellias provided the ladies of the family with corsages to adorn their Sunday and special- occasion dresses. Dad's flower-arranging skills provided center pieces for the church as well.

Chapter 6

OFF TO WORK
(Allen's story continued)

All the young men of the family went to work outside the home at an early age. Older brother Greg remembered working for a Mr. Rook in the peddling business. He'd buy butter and eggs from farmers. "Every Saturday," Greg remembered, "we'd kill chickens, hang them on the clothesline, dip them in boiling water, pluck the feathers, and pack them in ice. We'd go to Atlanta and sell butter, eggs, and chickens." Later, he worked for a man delivering bread—Betsy Ross bread. Brother Tom went to work at an early age at a bank.

Allen remembered his first job: When I worked for Carl Jordan (Alford Brothers Store) I'd stock shelves and carry out groceries for customers. One job we had was to open a big box of cigarettes and stamp each package. The

Jordans used to feed me whatever Carl's wife Della fixed for him. I remember eating her biscuits. Whatever I ate at the store they deducted from my pay. I drank a quart of milk a day and gained 25-30 pounds that summer. They were paying me $20.00 a week, but I'd take home $5.00. It was a general store. I bought my clothes there, my shoes— whatever I wanted.

The highlight of my summer was when I could lift a 100-pound sack of feed and load it into the back of a truck. I'd load it on to a hand-truck, then inch it up to the big truck. I worked there, summers and Saturdays until we moved to Atlanta.

One day Claude Garmon's dad came in and said, "I want a box of apple."

Carl said, "Get him a box of apple." So, I got a box of apples and put them in the back of his truck.

Mr. Garmon came back in the store later and asked, "Who put the box of apples in my truck?" They all looked at me, and I had nowhere else to look. They had to tell me to bring the apples back and give him a box of Apple chewing-tobacco.

When we lived in Atlanta, I worked for a time with my dad at the 7-11 in Sandy Springs, Georgia. The ice man would bring ice in 300-pound blocks. The block would be on the truck. The ice man would hook his pincers into the ice and slide it along the bed of the truck and into our own ice house. The construction workers would come in with coolers. They'd chip the ice into their coolers and pay for their ice supply.

I'd stock shelves and wait on customers. Dad worked 7 days a week, but I told him I had to go to church on Sunday.

Later I got a job working at A & P sacking groceries and mopping floors. We'd run all day—sacking and loading groceries. After sacking groceries (8:00 A. M.-7:00 P. M.), we'd organize the mopping crew. One would mop, one would rinse, and, when the floor was dry, someone else would follow with the wax mop. When we got out of there, I'd either go watch a movie, or go home and get a bath and go to bed.

Other times I'd socialize with guys I worked with at A & P. We'd hang out and go places together. Most often it would be a drive-in restaurant. We'd order ice cream floats.

The surface of my life seemed unruffled. But seeds sown early in my life would soon bring my life to its turning point.

Chapter 7

SPARED II

When I was about 8 years old, I would go to church and revival meetings at Gloster Baptist Church. The preacher, DeWitt Fowler, would preach hard and fast, and I'd stand in the pew weeping with conviction. Someone would ask, "Allen, what's wrong?"

"I don't know." I'd say.

The older I got, the less conviction I felt. In my young teens I no longer wept about my sin.

When we moved to Brookhaven and I started going to Brookhaven Baptist, it was an entirely different church environment. The preacher, W. T. Booth, preached the gospel—quietly but fervently. He was a fluent, polished preacher. Eventually, conviction returned.

One Sunday, conviction led me to weep. I felt that if I didn't get saved then, I never would. I walked down the aisle, and as I walked, I repented and received Christ as my Saviour. That was the turning point to which God's Spirit had been drawing me.

I was baptized two weeks later. Now I went to church Sunday morning, Sunday night, and Wednesday night. In Training Union, I began to speak before others. The teens would discuss Bible topics and current issues.

After church on Sunday night we'd go to someone's house and play games and have refreshments. One family named Gaines, who lived across the street from the church, often hosted the teens. Not only did the church provide the focal point for my social life, it also prompted me to reach out to others. After I got saved, I'd join others to go out and canvass the neighborhoods inviting people to church.

About a year later I remember being at home and thinking about wanting to serve the Lord. I remember reading the story of the call of Moses. I got down on my

knees and prayed about it, and the Lord impressed on my

heart that I should be a preacher.

Shortly after, I was visiting with my sister-in-law

Betty. We often walked together and talked about things.

She recalls, "We walked because he wanted to talk.

'I've got to tell you something,' he confided. 'I'm

going to be a pastor. I've never told anyone else. You're the

first one to know.' "

Later I went forward in church and told the

congregation, Allen recalled.

Our pastor was going on vacation. He asked me two

months earlier if I'd preach once while he was on vacation. I

said, "Yes." Then, just a day or two after he left, I had my

front teeth pulled. The assistant pastor asked me if I'd still

be able to preach and I told him, "Yes." The sermon was

titled "The Cross of Christ." I preached on a Sunday night,

then turned the service over to the assistant pastor.

Some time later I was asked to come back to Gloster

Baptist and preach. Ethel's boyfriend and Ethel took me to

the church. I remember thinking my sermon must not have

been very effective, because the preacher got up after me

and "exhorted" the people for as long as my sermon.

After graduation, I wanted to get some dental work

done and paid for before I went to college. My dad wanted

me to go to a dentist in Stone Mountain who was his cousin.

So I took a city bus to downtown Atlanta, then transferred to

a Stone Mountain bus. When the dentist told me what

needed to be done and what it would cost, I went to a bank

and borrowed the money, then continued working at A & P

to repay the loan.

After I repaid the loan, I quit my job and entered

Truett McConnell.

Chapter 8

MEANWHILE III

Meanwhile, the young lady 270 miles away was being drawn at an early age by the same Holy Spirit to a point that seemed more a starting point than a turning point in her life. Her earliest memories were of standing in the pew near the front of Friendship Baptist Church and weeping with conviction, not knowing why she was weeping.

With the children's crusade conducted at her church by Harold and Helen Alexander came an understanding: God was calling, and she needed to respond—to accept His offer of eternal life, to call on Him to save her. Still, she hesitated. The invitation had been given and the questions asked, "Have you trusted Christ? Have you called on Him to save you?" She stood with her hands by her side until she felt a nudge by her sister and obeyed the whispered

command, "Raise your hand."

Not until a later Monday night—March 19, 1951,

following a film series at her church the night before did

conviction lead to action. The film series featured three

films. One showed hot springs and volcanoes issuing from

the heart of the earth and suggesting a possible source for

the fire of God's judgment. Another told a story of "The

Man that Forgot God." The third depicted the second

coming of Christ.

It was the truth of the second coming of Christ that

led to action. She was lying in bed on that Monday evening

thinking about the second coming of Christ. The house was

quiet. Dad was at a deacon's meeting at church. Mom was

in the living room folding clothes. The children were all in

bed. She thought about her past plan of action, "If Jesus

comes back, I'll grab hold of Mom or Dad and go up with one

of them. I know God won't leave them behind." But now in

the quietness of the hour, a new thought entered her mind, "What if He comes now? I can't grab Mom or Dad. Neither of them is within reach." Then, an even more alarming thought, "What if He has come already and I am left behind?" She had to know.

Rising from bed, she tiptoed to the living room, where the sight of Mom folding clothes brought great relief. "Mom, I need to be saved," she confessed and bowed at her knees to call on the Saviour. Relief, like the weight of a piano being lifted from her shoulders, flooded her soul. Peace took the place of the unbearable weight. She was now God's child. She was now ready for His return. Her heart would forever be His.

This new love loosened the tongue of this most timid of all students to tell her third-grade teacher, "I got saved last night." She would forever after love to tell the story.

Not only did this love loosen her tongue, it also opened her ears to hear His call. Every message from God's

Word was His word to her. Every missionary challenge offered an exciting possibility of service to the One she loved.

Fellowship in her teens centered on church activities. A Thursday night Teen Night at the church offered recreation in a brightly-lit, well-chaperoned environment. The church teens also participated in a Youth for Christ rally on Saturday nights at the YMCA in downtown Charleston.

As graduation from high school drew near and the necessity of training for the service to which she felt God calling her loomed on the horizon, this student took her first steps toward seeking and following God's will. Visits to two college campuses had answered one question concerning God's direction for her life: Should she seek education at a secular or a Christian college?

Secular Winthrop College offered a beautiful campus—blanketed in snow when she saw it for the first time—her first sight of snow! Winthrop also offered scholarships to students who would commit to teaching in South Carolina for a given number of years. This she could not do, not knowing where God would lead after graduation.

A visit to Columbia Bible College for their spring Bible conference offered education in another dimension. Here, the Spirit of God presided over an education both heart-warming and soul-stirring as well as mentally challenging. Surely, this was the kind of education God had chosen for her.

Meanwhile, a men's quartet visiting her church from Tennessee Temple College had introduced her to the possibility of training there. Learning that the college offered work scholarships to students needing financial assistance made Temple seem a good choice. When her application for admission brought the offer of a tuition scholarship, the choice was made. The savings from her earnings during high school would pay her first year's room and board, and she would apply for a work scholarship thereafter.

As an added assurance that God would indeed meet all her needs—as His Word had assured her—God even provided transportation for her first semester at Temple. The parents of a young lady from the nearby town of Summerville inquired of her pastor to find another student headed to Temple and offered transportation. The adventure of following her Lord had begun!

Chapter 9

PREPARED
(Allen's story continued)

At Truett-McConnell I joined a group of students who went to a nursing home to visit the residents. During the week I would announce the ministry in the dining hall and recruit students to go with us every Sunday afternoon.

One Tuesday afternoon two or three of us guys were sitting on the lawn of the girls' dormitory across from the Methodist Church. A man drove up to the curb and asked if there were any preachers around. We told him we were preachers. He told us he wanted to have a revival meeting at his church near Clayton, Georgia, starting the following Sunday. We said, "Sure, we'll help you."

I preached one night, and the other guys preached one night each. The following Sunday I taught a Sunday School class of junior boys. On the second Sunday afternoon a fire started in the preacher's front yard. We were all

running around with buckets of water trying to put out the

fire.

During the revival one of the men invited us to

supper before church. He served a scrumptious meal. He'd

ask, "Would you like some of this?" We'd be busy talking

and not answer, so he'd help us to more food until we cried,

"No, that's enough! I can't eat anymore!"

Results of the revival were both temporal and

spiritual. Somebody re-dedicated his life to the Lord. And

all the college boys got girlfriends. We'd go up on Saturday

and stay to go to church on Sunday. On Sunday afternoons

we'd visit with the girls and then go back to campus.

I worked one summer at a cafe' in Cleveland,

Georgia. I cooked hamburgers, hot dogs, and French fries,

and waited tables. One day the owner sent me to put half a

case of eggs (30 dozen eggs) in the cooler. The next day she

let me have it: "Don't you know the difference between a

freezer and a cooler?" In my ignorance I had frozen 30 dozen eggs!

But college life had its lighter side as well. We lived in an H-shaped army barracks. In the middle hall were the showers—unheated. The guys would turn on the hot water to heat the shower rooms.

One night two pranksters decided to scare everyone. They put on rubber masks and dragged their feet down the hall, banging on doors and grunting. In one room the occupants refused to open the door, so the monsters took the door off the hinges. The boys jumped on their beds and screamed. I was following them around and laughing my head off.

On another occasion I was the victim of a prankster. We had bunk beds and a string in the middle of the room attached to the light. We tied more string to the original, then tied that string to the bed. On one occasion someone tied a dead animal to my light string. So I came in on a dark night and felt the furry creature instead of the string. I backed out of the room with a scream.

One guy named Gary bought a box of fig newtons and a box of Carter's little liver pills. He put the liver pills in the fig newtons, and offered them to other students. They were glad to get a sweet treat until they bit into one of the bitter liver pills.

Paying the school bill was always a challenge. One year the Eastern Star (the Ladies Auxiliary of the Masons) paid my bill. One quarter a Sunday School class of retired people paid my bill. One quarter a retired missionary paid my bill.

I had been called into the president's office and told I had to go home and get some money. I walked out to the road and hitchhiked to Atlanta. That evening when I got home, I called Al Buice. He came and took me to church. The pastor was a retired missionary. He had been a missionary in Africa and had come home to start churches in Georgia.

When I got to church, the pastor asked me, "What are you doing here? You're supposed to be in school." I told him they sent me home and told me not to come back until I could pay my bill. He took a church bulletin and wrote a note saying that he'd be responsible for the bill and asked them to let me back in school.

After my time at Truett-McConnell I transferred to Mercer University and attended one quarter. There was a National Guard Armory on campus. Students attended drinking parties there.

I had a roommate at Mercer who hurt his toe very badly—so badly it took the nail off. He lay in the bunk and groaned and cursed all night long. I decided this was not the place to prepare for ministry; I'd leave and go home, which I did the next day.

I had started having a persistent cough with a dark discharge before I left Truett-McConnell. I decided it was time to take care of this problem, so I went to the doctor in north Atlanta. He x-rayed my chest and sent me to Piedmont Hospital for tests. I told him I had no money. He told me it would be taken care of. The tests revealed bronchiectasis in my left lower lobe.

Treatment consisted of putting me to sleep and running a tube down my throat to try to extract the accumulated mucous and infection. I would wake up with a terrible sore throat. When these treatments failed to remove the infection, it was decided that surgery would be needed to remove the diseased left lower lobe.

I was sent home for two weeks, then went back for surgery. I prayed for God to heal me if it was His will, and if not to give me grace to go through the surgery.

I awoke in terrible pain. They had cut me from the center of my chest to the middle of my back and left the incision in stitches. I was there for two weeks before they

sent me home. I remember Pastor Booth from Brookhaven

Baptist coming to see me. Mary Brophy from Truett-

McConnell came to see me. A girl who had had the same

surgery came to see me and encouraged me that I would get

well and not to give up.

The Lord used that painful experience to draw me

closer to Himself and to motivate me to seek His will more

fervently. It also helped me be more compassionate toward

others who are suffering.

While I was in the hospital, my parents moved to

Chamblee. When I was recuperating, Al Buice, whom I had

met at Brookhaven Baptist, came and started taking me to

an independent Baptist church on Beufort Highway.

The pastor had a business, and several members

wanted him to leave his business and pastor full time. He

refused. So several members left the church and organized

an independent Baptist church which met in someone's

home. They called Grady Sanford as pastor. They bought property in Norcross, Georgia, built a basement, and started meeting in the basement.

Al Buice's brother Charles came to visit the church. He told us about Temple, and I decided I'd visit. I had also heard about Temple at Youth for Christ rallies. Nancy Ball would come to Youth for Christ rallies and give her testimony about Temple.

In the summer of '63 I planned to visit both Temple and Bryan College. My brother Tom was to take me. But on the day appointed, my brother overslept. I called him, and he was just getting up. Instead, I caught a bus in downtown Atlanta and rode to Chattanooga.

When I got to Chattanooga, they were having a summer Bible conference. As I listened to the preachers (among them William Ward Ayre) I decided this was where I needed to be.

I believe that's how the Lord works. If you leave the choice to Him, He will eliminate all choices but one, so that you will know His will.

I had been working about a year after recovering from surgery, stacking paper from a cutter at a paper-products factory. I went back to work and gave them my notice. One of the men at church told me, "You're foolish to leave a good job and go to school."

I had given my application to Dr. Lockery, Temple's registrar, before I left Temple. I went to school with one week's pay in my pocket. With that $50.00 I bought books, paper, and pens, and started classes. Several weeks after I had started classes I got a notice from Dr. Lockery's office telling me that I had been accepted.

I started looking for a job through the employment office. One day I met Charles Buice in front of the Happy Corner. He asked me, "Would you do anything to pay your school bill?"

"Yes, I would," I answered.

Then he told me that Erlanger Hospital was hiring. So I went to Erlanger Hospital and filled out an application, and they hired me for an orderly on the night shift. We were basically nurses' assistants. Whatever the nurses told us to do, we did it: take temperature, pulse, and respiration; bathe patients; change bed linens; etc.

Shortly after I started working at Erlanger, I met a couple named Saunders. They were both nurses on the night shift. He worked for the hospital, and she was a private duty nurse. They lived in Highland Park and provided me transportation to work and back to school.

I made enough money to pay my school bill weekly and have $5.00 left over. With that $5.00 I bought tooth paste, razor blades, and other necessities, and did my laundry. When I graduated from Temple, I didn't owe anybody anything.

Erlanger offered some unique learning experiences. The first patient I attended with delirium tremens was a man who had been in a car accident and had broken both legs. He was brought to the orthopedic ward with both legs in a cast. We didn't know he was an alcoholic until he started thrashing about the bed and had to be restrained. He could not talk coherently. After one night of tending this man, I didn't see him any more: he was moved to the psychiatric ward.

Death was an occasional visitor. One unit at Erlanger had an old man in a bed in the hall. He was ranting and raving. Another orderly and I were assigned to watch him and restrain him if necessary. He opened a safety pin and threatened to attack us if we came close. The other orderly was able to grab his hand, and I helped hold him down. After about 5-10 minutes of restraining him, his straining stopped and he went limp. He had died of a heart attack.

One night I was working in the emergency room. The doctors and nurses were working on a man who was struggling to breathe. He turned red, then purple, then stopped struggling and turned pink again. He had died.

On one occasion I witnessed a birth. I was working in the isolation ward, which overlooked the emergency room entrance. From a window I heard a cab drive up to the emergency room entrance and blow its horn. Some emergency room personnel ran out to help a woman out of the cab. She was delivering a baby. The baby was born into the doctor's hands. They took the purple newborn into the emergency room.

When I was working in the emergency room, I had the biggest scare of the job when I was sent one night to deliver a patient to the delivery room. I feared she would deliver the baby on the elevator going up—with no one but me to attend.

No doubt the experience I got at Erlanger was part of God's plan to prepare me for a ministry of caring for others.

Church at Highland Park, chapel, and classes at Temple were the golden years of my life: the joy of Bible teaching, the fellowship of fellow students who loved the Lord, the delight of a personal walk with the Lord.

Chapter 10

PAIRED

A special glow enhanced those golden years when I began to court a young lady whom I met there at Temple. I had first dated her roommate Ruth Kraus. Ruth said to me, "You ought to date my roommate."

"What's her name?" I asked. She told me the name, then wrote it down for me—first and last name.

One day I saw her in the lobby of the student center and introduced myself. Soon we were together in the cafeteria, in chapel, in church, in the library, at concerts, at basketball games. Occasionally we escaped campus to explore the beautiful Chattanooga countryside. Sunset Rock on Lookout Mountain and Cloudland Canyon provided favorite getaways. These shared experiences—always chaperoned—laid a foundation of companionship for our developing relationship.

My observations during those days were of a young lady working cheerfully in the dining hall, studying diligently in the library, practicing faithfully in the practice rooms. These observations helped complete the transformation that the Holy Spirit was making in my own attitude toward work, and my school work in particular. I had drifted through high school with a careless attitude toward work, barely passing. Now I was confronted with a challenge that required a dedication to the task that I had not previously known. Evangelism class, for example, required memorization of 8-10 verses a week. I was failing every week when the Lord convicted me that I could do better. I began to learn those verses and went from F's to A's in one week.

Jennie's devotion to excellence in her work inspired a similar devotion in me. I could see that she was dedicated to being prepared for the Lord's service, and I wanted to be

well prepared also.

The ministries we shared bound our hearts together

for future ministry. Our ministry at Temple began with an

invitation to ride the bus to the Children's Home and sit with

the children in church. As their warm bodies wiggled next to

ours in church, we experienced the joy of sharing with

others the love God had so graciously given to us.

On a Sunday afternoon in December of 1963, Jennie

and I walked to a pond in Jennie's neighborhood and there I

proposed marriage. Jennie's consent sealed our

engagement. I had prayed at the age of eighteen that God

would give me a Christian wife, and now, at the age of 24,

God was answering my prayer. Later that evening her dad

gave his consent. In the meantime we attended a wedding

at Friendship Baptist Church, where we would stand before

the same pastor in June of 1965 and exchange our vows.

In a whirlwind week of activities, Jennie graduated from Tennessee Temple College on a Monday evening in May of 1965, attended a bridal shower at her home church on Thursday evening, and our wedding rehearsal on Friday evening. We were married that Saturday evening, June 5, 1965—evening because Dad was working and wouldn't leave the barber shop until closing time.

My brother Greg, his wife and three girls had come to represent the Britt family. My roommate Cloyd Young had come to be my best man. Jennie's brother Tony, her cousin David, her sister Lottie, and friends Jackie Knowles and Judy Young completed the wedding party. Second cousins Eugene and Donna Burns were ring bearer and flower girl. They added a bit of excitement when Eugene started the arch swinging over our heads. Jennie's attempt to put my ring on the wrong hand gave us a tense moment then and laughter later. Our wedding song, "In shady green pastures so rich and so sweet God leads his dear children along . . ." was our testimony then and continued to be through the years.

After the reception Cousin David took us to the Francis Marion Hotel in downtown Charleston for our overnight honeymoon. By Monday we were boarding a bus for Chattanooga where I resumed my work at Erlanger Hospital and my studies at Tennessee Temple.

Soon after we were married M. J. Parker came to our apartment on Union Avenue with an invitation to attend the bus pastor's meeting on Saturday morning and start working a bus route. Soon we were knocking on doors every Saturday and riding the bus every Sunday. The Highland Park bus route was our first assignment.

By the time we started working the bus route, I had left Erlanger and gone to work at C. D. Genter, a manufacturer of leather gloves. My job was separating the leather into like colors. I rode to work with Faye Curtis, another student from Temple. As soon as classes were over,

we left for work, and came home about 7:30 or 8:00 P. M.

Meanwhile, Jennie had found a position at the UTC

(University of Tennessee at Chattanooga) Library working in

the reference library as a graduate assistant. This position

paid her tuition to begin studies in the graduate program.

She worked days while I attended classes.

Saturdays we worked together on the bus route. The

bus ministry was my first experience of door-to-door

visitation. We visited the regulars every week and

encouraged them as well as seeking new riders.

One day I told Parker about a man on our route who

was lost. "Let's go see him," he said. We traveled in

Parker's Dodge Dart to the address on Vance Avenue. We

knocked on the door, and the man invited us in. Parker

started to witness to him, then asked him if he wanted to be

saved. The man said, "Yes, but I can't be saved at home, I

have to be in church." So Parker put him in his car and

drove him to Highland Park Baptist Church—and led him to Christ at the altar.

I was with Parker another time when we visited a lady who said, "I can't come to church. I don't have a dress to wear."

Parker said, "I've got a dress you can wear," and went to the car, brought back a dress, and pulled it over the clothes she was wearing. It fit perfectly! Now she had no excuse.

Parker was a legendary figure in the bus ministry. He inspired me to be aggressive in seeking the lost and bringing people in to God's house. His compassion was the motivating compulsion of his life. He lived for others.

Among our regulars on the bus route was the unforgettable Emma Marsh. She would always tell me when she got off the bus on a Sunday afternoon, "Don't come for me. I'm not coming back any more. I'm quitting."

We'd visit her on Saturday and when we left she'd say, "Be sure and stop for me tomorrow."

When Emma met another of our regulars, Mary Christmas, Mary told her her name and Emma said, "Glad to meet you. I'm Happy New Year."

Regulars ran the economic gamut from the children of impoverished families to the lady who had her own drapery business. Domestic scenes ran the gamut from scenes of squalor to scenes of domestic tranquility. All became "family."

One little fellow won a special place in our hearts. Douglas Dial moved into Highland Park with his mother and sister from another bus route. As soon as those big brown eyes met ours, Douglas went straight to our hearts. We wanted to care for Douglas and make him our own. We <u>did</u> ask his mom if he could spend the night, but we never mustered the nerve to ask if we could adopt him.

Not long after Douglas came into our lives, God gave us another Douglas that we could care for for a short time. Douglas Horne, my nephew, needed a home for part of the time his dad was in Viet Nam. When we were asked to take him in, we were excited about the opportunity. We drove to Atlanta and brought him back with us.

After going to the phone one day, calling "Mom?" and hearing no answer, Douglas began calling Jennie "Mom." But he was essentially a Daddy's boy. He came to me immediately when we went to pick him up and always followed me to the door when I had to leave, climbing into a chair and watching as long as he could see me.

Our hearts were wrenched when his dad came to get him. We never saw Douglas again. We were sent one picture and one letter, but Douglas remained the darling of our hearts until his early death some years later from complications resulting from a car accident.

During the transition time before we left Highland Park, with graduation just a few weeks away, I was asked to train someone else for our bus route and work on the other bus routes.

One week-end we visited with Carl & Dotty Bieber a bus route in Ooletewah, Tennessee. Someone wearing overalls and a baseball cap with hair curling about the neck and a light growth of beard was standing in the yard. I asked, "Where does this gentleman go to church?" Carl was standing behind me and shaking his head, trying to tell me that this was not a gentleman.

The person spoke—in a deep bass voice—and said, "I don't go to church anywhere." Only later did I learn that I had stuck my foot in my mouth.

Life was full of surprises. One Sunday morning in East Chattanooga the bus stopped to avoid hitting a small object in the road. I got out and saw a small child sitting in the street in a diaper. I picked him up, then looked around to see where he belonged. No one was in sight, but there was a house with a door open. Assuming he had opened the door himself and toddled into the street, I took him to the door and set him down inside.

After a semester working as a graduate assistant in the reference library, Jennie had dropped her hours in the graduate program and taken a job babysitting for a couple attending Temple. At the end of that semester, she had done her student teaching in the summer school at Rossville High School. Now she was teaching in the same county— Walker County, Georgia—teaching 7th & 8th grade English at Rock Springs Elementary School in Rock Springs, Georgia.

With graduation approaching, we were praying about what to do after graduation. Carl Bieber kept saying to us, "Come go to Elkton with me. I need teachers." Carl had already been called to come to Elkton and serve as school principal. He was currently fulfilling Tom Wallace's requirement that he first go to Temple and study the

Christian philosophy of education. He made arrangements

for Tom Wallace to interview us when he came to Bible

Conference that year. We met on campus and talked about

what he wanted me to do. He was offering me a ministry as

visitation director at Baptist Bible Church. I felt peace that

this was what God wanted me to do. Jennie would teach in

the Christian school.

Twins: Hellen (l.) and Allen (r.) born May 17, 1939

Dramatic Club 1

High School Drama Club, Chamblee High School,

1957

ALLEN R. BRITT
ATLANTA, GA.
I know what's what.

Missionary Volunteers; Music Club;
Messianic Fellowship.

Tennessee Temple Bible School,

1965

Wedding Day-June 5, 1965

Uncle Allen with nephew Douglas

Lookout Mountain, 1968

"Man Friday" at work ????

Bible Baptist-Elkton, Maryland

1971

Andrew Allen Britt, born October 1, 1974

Family/School Photo-Barbour Christian Academy,

1985

Family/School Photo-Barbour Christian Academy,

1988

The Empty Nest, 2003

Grandpa with son Andrew and Grandson Drew,

1997

Grandpa with Grandson Dalton

Father's Day, 2007

An Old-Fashioned Preacher-Faith Baptist

Chapter 11

SHARED

Here was the opportunity for which we had

prepared. I would share my faith in the community. Jennie

would share her skills in the classroom.

From a fellow student who ran a used-furniture

business in Chattanooga, we bought a bedroom set to

furnish the apartment we had been promised in Elkton.

From the state of Georgia we withdrew the funds

accumulated in Jennie's retirement fund to rent a U-Haul to

move our belongings to Elkton.

Moving day was unforgettable. We were driving a

Chevrolet and pulling a U-Haul trailer with all our earthly

possessions—including the bedroom set we had just bought

from Mack Johnson. We decided to exit Interstate 81 at

Pulaski, Virginia, not knowing that we had chosen the route

over the mountain. When we started down the mountain, the brakes began to fail. I had to shift to lower gears to control the speed. With careful shifting and much praying we pulled into Pulaski, found a mechanic to work on the car, then a place to spend the night. Next day we were on our way with new brakes and high hopes for a safe conclusion to our journey.

As we approached Baltimore the next day in a driving rain, we missed our exit, not once but twice—once driving through the city to find our way, the second time driving completely around it. We would come right up to the signs and not be able to read them for the blinding sheets of rain. We did finally arrive safely at our destination on a Saturday night, somewhat later than anticipated.

We were moved into an attic apartment that the church had rented for us—one bedroom, living room, kitchen—all under the eaves, all heated by the sun so that when you climbed the stairs in summer you felt like you were walking into an oven. The water was a beautiful blue-green, tinting all the fixtures and tainting the taste so that it was only palatable when made into tea.

After several visits to other churches—preaching at Beulah Baptist in Oxford, Pennsylvania, and People's Baptist in Frederick, Maryland, among others—we settled into the work at Baptist Bible: teaching for Jennie, visitation and overseeing the children's church for me.

My early visitation efforts seemed fruitless, finding few people at home and fewer willing to talk. Then the Lord brought a compatible visitation partner into my life. Linwood Cahall was a unique individual, willing to go anywhere, capable of making anyone feel comfortable. He would take me to see the up and out and the down and out.

His homespun, down-to-earth interest in others put everyone at ease.

Among the up and out he took me to see was a man who lived near the Methodist Church in Elk Mills. We stood in his yard one spring day and talked to him about his soul. When asked if he were going to Heaven when he died, he said, "Yes, I'm going to Heaven." He pointed to the Methodist Church and added, "I built that church." His mind was closed to the gospel. He couldn't believe he needed to trust Christ. He believed his good works would get him to Heaven.

Cahall and I went to see a middle-aged couple that Cahall knew living on Route 7 in a modest frame house. After we explained the gospel to them, they said, "We're not ready. You come back after Christmas." We tried to persuade them to trust Christ now, but to no avail.

Jennie and I went to Charleston for Christmas. When we came back after Christmas, Cahall told me this couple hath both been killed in a car accident. They had pulled into Route 40 from Route 7, and a truck had hit their car.

An older man we visited on Dogwood Road was very ill. Someone let us in on a cold winter day, then left us in a boiling hot room with the sickening odor of disease and death. Cahall got sick and had to leave. The man told me he was lost and he wanted to be saved. I was getting sick too, but I determined to stay and explain the gospel to him. He prayed to receive Christ and we left. We learned later that he had died within two weeks of our visit.

On Route 7 toward North East we visited an older man who was bedridden. We led him to the Lord and talked to him about baptism. He said he didn't think he could be baptized, but he didn't reckon with the determination of Linwood Cahall. Cahall arranged a stretcher to bring him to church and a chair to baptize him in.

One day Cahall and I were out visiting on Appleton Road. We passed a service station where a young girl was standing near a car. A man nearby lit a cigarette and tossed the match to the ground. Suddenly she was engulfed in flames that burnt her clothes off. Someone from the service station wrapped her in a blanket. She was walking around and complaining that she was losing the feeling in her legs. We visited her later in the hospital where she died from infection in a matter of weeks.

Dogs were an occupational hazard of door-to-door visitation. Cahall and I were visiting on Route 7 and knocked on a door. The door opened and a little yappity dog came out. We talked to the resident on the porch, and then left. As we were walking down the sidewalk toward the car, the dog ran after us, yapping all the while. A sharp pain told me he had nipped me on my ankle bone.

That dog had not aroused any fear, but other dogs did. One day I traveled down a long lane to a lone house at the end of the lane. I parked the car and started walking toward the house. As I approached the house, a huge St.

Bernard started lumbering toward me. In my great wisdom, I turned and ran back to the car and closed the door behind me.

The St. Bernard followed me to the car, bracing his paws against the window and dropping his mouth open to show me its toothless interior. I still wonder: Was it a toothless greeting or a toothless grin?

Jennie and I visited together on church bus routes. Once Jennie and I were visiting on the Chesapeake bus route. We parked the car in somebody's yard and walked to the door of the porch. When I attempted to open the door, a big German shepherd bounded toward me with a threatening bark. I slammed the door on his muzzle, and his bark changed to a whimper. We made a hasty departure to the car.

It was a varied ministry—school teaching for Jennie, visitation for me, the bus route for us both. Sunday morning found us working together in Sunday School, then children's church. On one occasion we were asked to help haunt the

Russell farm for a teen event. We dressed as a headless

corpse—Jennie representing the corpse, lying on a board

supported by bales of hay. I lay beneath the board between

the bales of hay to represent the head. An occasional

thrashing of a leg represented the dying throes of the

"body." Visiting spiders haunted the "head," while the

passing teens seemed only slightly amused.

Elkton exemplified the term "church family" in its

finest sense. Church families took us into their hearts and

into their homes. Warren and Pat Perry, Jim and Judy

Paynter, Denneys, Barnetts—all invited us into their homes,

once for an overnight as well as an evening visit. And their

children were welcomed into our home when the

opportunity called: mom in the hospital, mom and dad

away at church camp. With one co-worker, Martha Jacobs,

Jennie shared her first-ever sledding adventure!

One young man in the Christian school became part of our family for part of his high school career. Brian Rebert lived in Hanover, Pennsylvania, and drove to Elkton, Maryland to attend Elkton Christian Schools Monday-Friday. For the evenings of his stay in Elkton he roomed with us and became part of our family. Many of the friendships developed there in Elkton became treasured friends for life.

In our third year in Elkton we learned that Pastor Tom Wallace had accepted a call to Beth Haven Baptist Church in Louisville, Kentucky. We worked with the new pastor Tom Berry for a year before accepting a call to Mountain Lake Independent Baptist in Oakland, Maryland.

Chapter 12

SHARED II

Oakland was a very fruitful ministry. I began preaching there in May of 1972—three times weekly in the church and once a week on the radio. The radio program had been called Mountaintop Meditations. I changed the name to Help from the Hills but continued the devotional theme.

Visitation—for the most part—consisted of following names given me by church members. Many of these names came from a faithful bus pastor and his wife. One evening I went to see a man right outside of town on Route 135. We sat in his living room, and I explained the gospel to him, then asked him if he wanted to be saved. He said he wasn't ready yet, but he let me pray with him.

The next Sunday morning after the message, someone brought a little boy forward to make a public profession of faith. The little boy was the 10-year-old son of the man to whom I had witnessed. Unknown to me, he had been standing behind a door and listening to my witness. He had prayed then and asked the Lord to save him.

Another time I went to Bradley Manor community and knocked on a door. I was invited in and after a brief visit began giving the gospel. While I was giving the gospel, the man got up and walked out. When I saw him outside talking to someone in the parking lot, I realized he was not interested.

Somebody had given me the name of an old Italian man. So I took Jennie home after church on a Sunday afternoon and drove out to the man's house. I knocked on the door and asked for the man by name. They told me that I could talk to him, but I'd have to talk loud because he was hard of hearing. I talked to him and got acquainted. Then I began to witness. He wanted to be saved and so he prayed

to receive Christ. He was 99 years old.

The next day I decided I'd like to go back and see

him. I went to the house and it was empty. While I was

witnessing to the man the day before, the family had been

packing and getting ready to move. By the time I arrived the

next day, they had gone.

We baptized at a non-denominational Bible church in

Terra Alta, West Virginia, 11 miles west of Oakland. We

were told someone would run warm water into the baptistry

the night before we baptized. By the time we arrived the

next day, the water would be ice cold.

On a cold Sunday afternoon we drove to Terra Alta to

baptize Mrs. Durst. She and I walked slowly into the water.

I held out my hand to steady her. After pronouncing the

words, "Because of your profession of faith in Christ Jesus, I

baptize you in the name of the Father and of the Son and of

the Holy Spirit," I lowered her into the water. She came up with a gasp that told everyone, "That was COLD water."

The bus pastor had led a young man named Eddie to the Lord. Eddie was a rather large young man whom everyone called "Little Eddie." He came forward in a church service for public profession and baptism. When we arrived at Terra Alta for the baptism, Don Williams asked me, "Do you need any help?"

In my self-confidence and ignorance, I replied, "No, I don't need any help." Well, I didn't need any help getting Eddie down, but when I tried to bring him up, he slipped out of my hands and thrashed about a bit before recovering his balance. I thought I had lost him, and I thought I was going under with him.

One of the duties that fell to the pastor of Mountain Lake Independent Baptist Church was to take the children who had completed the Bible Memory program for the year to the Bible Memory Association camp in Cleveland,

Georgia. We drove a station wagon loaded with campers and luggage over the mountains to Cleveland. Frequent stops for the relief of the carsick make it a memorable occasion.

On another occasion we drove over the mountains to St. George, West Virginia, to take Leila Pifer to visit her family. It was Jennie's first time to see a wood stove used for cooking, for heating the house, and for heating water. The water was heated in a reservoir on one side of the stove. At the time we had no idea that we would one day live and work in West Virginia.

Our lives in Oakland, however, did have a link to West Virginia. We learned early in the ministry in Oakland that two of the church families had grown children in Kingwood, West Virginia, and that there was no independent Baptist church there. We began meeting with these two women and others interested in starting a church in Kingwood. For many months we met in the home of a

Mrs. Kern for Bible study. Part of the time Jennie held a

Bible club for children in another home.

Among the ladies who attended the Bible study was

Bertie Marshall, who drove into Kingwood from her home in

Tunnelton. Through her we eventually met her sons John

and Allen. John was an evangelist, traveling with his family

in a remodeled bus which they used for a motor home.

Allen was to inherit his mother's property and develop it

into Wildwood Christian camp.

Oakland was a beautiful place to live. We enjoyed

the mountains all around. We enjoyed going every August

to pick blueberries on Mount Storm. We enjoyed the

beautiful valley where the Amish farmers lived. We enjoyed

the luscious whole milk we bought from the Amish people—

so rich Jennie could pour a whole pitcher of cream off the

top, and it was still so rich it tasted like a milkshake!

We enjoyed the beautiful view from the side of the

hill where we lived. Neighbors on both sides had children.

On one occasion I was called out of the house to retrieve a little boy who had climbed a tree and couldn't get down. Although out of practice as a tree climber, I managed to reach him and talk him down.

When the snow came, we enjoyed it from indoors. These people were accustomed to deep snow. They told us stories of winters past when drifts would be up to the telephone lines! We never closed services for snow.

One Sunday morning a heavy snowfall left us snow-bound. Don Williams, one of the deacons, stopped on the road below the house to pick us up for services. We were wading through the snow drifts toward his car when Jennie stepped into a drift up to her waist. Seventeen people arrived for services that day, including the family from Horse Shoe Run, West Virginia.

Even though meat prices sky-rocketed while we were in Oakland, we were well supplied with meat by members of the congregation. God had used ravens to feed Elijah. On another occasion he had sent an angel to feed Elijah. Now

he was using His saints to feed us.

It was also in Oakland that Jennie learned to bake

bread. Her mom and dad, sister Lottie, and her two boys

came for a visit. While they were there, Lottie taught her

sister to bake bread. Bread-making became a life-long

avocation.

It was also during this visit that Jennie's mom and

dad taught us to identify the elderberries growing on the

side of the road in abundance. They supplied us with our

favorite jelly to eat with our homemade whole wheat

bread—elderberry jelly!

On another occasion Jennie's brother Tony visited.

While he was there, Jennie noticed the first blooms from the

bulbs she had planted in front of the house. "Look at this!"

she exclaimed, jumping onto the front landing to reach the

blossoms on the other side. As she did, her feet slipped out

from under her and she landed on her seat.

"Yes, that's a neat trick," responded Tony, watching from the doorway.

When we left the ministry in Oakland, we considered moving to Kingwood to start a church there. While we were considering this possibility, however, another man arrived on the scene and expressed an interest in the Kingwood work. Eventually we felt led to leave the group in his hands and move on.

Chapter 13

SHARED III

We learned about a missionary pastor starting a church in Grafton, West Virginia, and decided to attend there when we left Oakland. They were a congregation of approximately 40 meeting in a large, old house on Lincoln Street (U. S. 119) in Grafton. Soon we were involved in this exciting new ministry—teaching Sunday School, visiting, driving the long 66-passenger bus. Without power steering, the bus required several stops and starts to maneuver it around the steep Grafton turns. Visitation, too, presented a physical challenge with many steps to climb on the steep hillsides.

We had been attending church in Grafton for just a short time when we learned about a ministry opportunity in Clarksburg, West Virginia. Emmanuel Christian School was in need of teachers. The missionary pastor in Grafton,

Norris Ward, arranged for us to be interviewed in Grafton on

the second Sunday night of our attendance there. The

school principal, Mrs. Mary Rosenau, came to Grafton with

her sister and brother-in-law, Ron Comfort. We felt that this

was God's open door for us and accepted the invitation to

teach. We were soon teaching and living in Ron Comfort's

home while we waited for the house we had arranged to

rent to become available.

On a typical Sunday in Grafton we would drive to

Grafton with our dinner aboard, teach Sunday School, help

where needed in the morning services (song leading for

Allen, nursery for Jennie), then share dinner with the Wards.

After dinner, we would find a place to rest, then resume

activities for the evening service.

One Sunday morning an early morning call from Ann

Ward informed us that her husband had been seriously

burned in an explosion when he went downstairs to light the

gas heater in an outside building. His polyester suit had

melted and saved him from more extensive burns, but he

had been hospitalized and needed me to take the services. I

was glad to teach Sunday School, lead the singing, and

preach morning and evening. When I visited Norris in the

hospital he was heavily bandaged and suffering drug-

induced spiritual oppression because of the pain medicine.

He did recover fully and returned to the pulpit within a few

weeks.

Norris mentioned to me that he would like to start

Bible studies in other towns in the hopes that they would

develop into new churches. Philippi was mentioned as a

possibility. While I thought about his suggestion, the Lord

began to prompt me to think about starting a church.

Meanwhile, our days were busy—teaching

combination classes third through eighth grade in Emmanuel

Christian School. I taught Bible and history. Jennie taught

grammar, literature, and language arts. This was my first

teaching experience, Jennie's first teaching combination

classes. Thursday afternoons kept us tied to our desks for

long planning sessions.

We did, however, make time to visit several of the

school families:

Lynches, who lived in a hollow at THE END of the

road. Their big-footed horses pulled us over the field on a

home-made sled!

Furners, where we saw the first peacocks we had

seen living in the wild.

Petermans, whose baby brother later blessed our

son with clothes he had outgrown.

In our second year at Emmanuel, Jennie's brother

Tony came to teach in the Christian school. Tony's presence

added a lot of fun—with his tendency to puns—and a lot of

music to our home. He was always practicing—piano, flute,

violin, recorder, or trumpet. Tony had just finished his

enlistment in the army, where he played a fife and wore a white-powdered wig in the Old Guard Fife and Drum Corps.

It was also in our second year at Emmanuel that a permanent addition to our family arrived. His arrival answered a long-standing prayer and fulfilled a long-cherished desire. We were elated when we learned of the impending birth.

We thought the Lord was preparing us for a girl because we had become so fond of the little girls in the church in Grafton—the sisters from the bus route who spent the night with us, the Christian school student who bathed and put on a clean dress for Wednesday night services so that she could spend the night and go to school with us the next day. Yet, we were delighted when we learned on October 1, 1974, that God had chosen to give us a baby boy.

What a thrill to bring him home to the big house on Pride Avenue in Clarksburg—in a dresser drawer. The house was soon equipped with the appurtenances of babyhood—

the washer and dryer Jennie's mom insisted we must have, the crib Jennie's dad bought for the new addition, the porta-crib one of the school families donated to the cause. The school families were nearly as excited as we were. They gave us a baby shower which supplied us with nearly everything needed—clothes, bedding, a humidifier, and enough money to buy his dresser.

Days were filled with delight—feeding, bathing, playtime. Jennie took a short leave to adjust to the new responsibilities. Dad went back to work. His favorite delight was to come home and nap with baby Andrew on his chest.

When Jennie returned to school, it was part time. She stayed home mornings to take care of the baby, wash diapers, sterilize bottles, then took him for afternoon care to a neighbor who was the mother of two of our Christian school students. Granny Calvert dearly loved our little bundle of joy, as did the folks in Grafton. They called him "The Jolly Green Giant"—jolly for his pleasant disposition, green for the green snowsuit he wore in winter, and giant because he was a big baby!

He was a good baby and a healthy baby—eating heartily, sleeping soundly, playing contentedly, and rarely crying. The only occasion that always brought a cry of protest was when brother Tony practiced the trumpet. Even when Tony went into the bathroom and closed the door to practice, Andy cried. When Tony practiced any other instrument—violin, piano, flute—Andy followed him with his eyes.

Andy was old enough to sit up when he suffered the only serious injury of his life. Jennie had brought him to the kitchen table to feed him breakfast when he plopped his hand into a plate of hot grits and suffered second degree burns. He cried much that day and we suffered with him. God sent an angel of mercy (Granny Calvert's daughter) to salve and bandage his burned hand, and he recovered splendidly.

It was also at this kitchen table that Andy got his first haircut. Jennie held one hand against his chest and with the other snipped the strands that straggled over his neck.

And it was at this kitchen table that we heard him laugh for the first time. Tony was entertaining us with a spastic clap, his hands aiming at one another and missing. Andy chuckled with a genuine whole body laugh that we never forgot.

We had decided that at the end of that year of school (1974-'75) Jennie would stay home and care for Andy until he was old enough to go to school. She was always glad she had—from the first day I went back to school. At eleven months, Andy took his first step on that day!

Andy also joined us in visiting school families:

Kinseys, where Andy drank from a cup for the first time. When Mrs. Kinsey was told, "No," in answer to her question whether he drank from a cup or not, she replied, "Wait and see."

Hursts, where our son ate spaghetti for the first time.

When Mrs. Hurst asked, "Would he like some?" and was

told, "I don't think so," she, too, let him decide for himself!

Chris Hall, whose adorable baby sister grew up to a

choir director at Emmanuel; and

Brummetts, who lived in the log cabin on the creek in

Grafton.

By the time we left Clarksburg the following year, he

was not only walking, but climbing everything available: the

steps to the basement garage, the steps to the slide in the

North View park across the street, the slide itself. On

moving day, Andy watched as the furniture was loaded onto

a truck, then wandered from room to room saying in the

most puzzled tone, "Gone, Gone, Gone."

Chapter 14

SHARED IV

My interest in Philippi started with Norris Ward's suggestion to begin a Bible study there. As I thought about his suggestion, the Holy Spirit prompted me to start a church instead. The first step was to look for a building to meet in. One visitation night in Grafton someone from the Grafton church sent me to Philippi to visit a friend in the Broaddus Hospital. After the visit I decided to go into the town to look for a meeting place. I had already inquired and had been turned down by the VFW and the public schools. I drove into town, crossed the Tygart River on Walnut Street, and on my right saw a huge empty building at 215 N. Walnut Street. I pulled into the driveway, stopped the car, and knocked on a neighbor's door to inquire. They told me who owned the building and where he lived.

On a Saturday morning that spring Jennie went with me through Belington on Route 250 South toward Elkins. We turned left onto a shale road and found Mr. Ketcham, the owner of the building in Philippi. That day we made arrangements to rent his building for church services.

In anticipation of holding services we needed to furnish the building. The church at West Milford, where I had preached many times, donated a sturdy, paneled pulpit and a set of pews. A piano for our use was loaned by a friend. Joe Harrah from Buckhannon donated hymn books. We were ready to begin. The date was set for the first Sunday in May of 1975.

With the help of Fred Barber from West Milford we designed and printed a flyer. Margaret Watkins, Mary Johnson, and others from the church in Grafton helped distribute flyers. John Winstead suggested we pray for 20 people.

With help from our Grafton friends we had pretty much covered the town with flyers when opening day came in May of 1975. Among the 22 people who assembled for that first service were Sharon Roe and her children. Sharon told us she had prayed for an independent Baptist church in Philippi. We felt that God had answered her prayers as well as ours.

Among those contacted by the flyer distribution were Forrest Bartlett, 88 years old at the time, and Mary Reynolds, also an octogenarian. Both began attending services at New Testament Baptist. Forrest Bartlett, we learned, had been saved for years but never baptized. Mary Reynolds was saved later in our revival meeting with Charlie Hicks. Both were baptized in our first baptism in the river at Moatsville Junction.

Early in that summer of 1975 Bennett Collins contacted me and asked if he could come and bring his tent for a meeting. I picked a site at Hacker Creek on Route 119

North. I was told that the property belonged to Jimbo Mayle and that I could find him at the Eagle Café. This was my first excursion into a drinking establishment, but I secured permission to use the property.

We had planned to put the tent up on the Saturday before the meetings. People from the Grafton Church had come to help. It was a cloudy day, and as soon as we got the tent up, the clouds burst into rain. While I was thinking, "I need to feed these people," Merrold Sams and his wife showed up with the food they had prepared for a picnic that got rained out. I had never seen stuffed peppers before, but I rejoiced to see them that day!

During the tent meeting we had a different crowd every night. They were Pentecostal people, expecting healing lines and whatever other attractions Pentecostal meetings offer. When they did not find their expectations met, they didn't come back. The tent meetings, however, did bring one couple who stayed with us: Wilda and Carl

Lanham from the local Methodist church. They had been saved previously and baptized by immersion. They had become acquainted with fundamental Bible preaching through the radio preaching of Oliver B. Greene and Jerry Falwell, and through reading the Sword of the Lord.

In the fall of that first year Evangelist Charles Hicks, a Tennessee Temple graduate, preached our first in-house revival. It was during this revival that our friend Mary Reynolds trusted Christ. Wilda Lanham's mom and dad, Clayton & Flora Fridley, Wilda's brother Jim, and Wilda's Uncle Ike Fridley all began attending during this meeting.

Here is Wilda's story, as she recalls it:

"Carl had become disenchanted with the Methodist Church by the time we saw the ad for New Testament Baptist Church in the Barbour Democrat. We came looking for it the first Sunday, but didn't find it. The second or third Sunday night we did find it. Jennie was sitting on the front seat. Little Andy was in a car seat. One of you (Pastor or

Jennie) loaned us a Bible. Pastor preached on Job 1:6-8.

'Satan,' Pastor preached, 'can go up and down in the earth,

but only God is omnipresent.'

"After that night we never came without our Bibles.

We joined during the Hicks revival. . . .

"I had given Dad a tape of J. Harold Smith's 'God's

Three Deadlines,' and he had asked the Lord to save him as

a result. Mom had been saved at Mount Olive Baptist

Church when I was 16 or 17. They both came forward to

make public professions of faith. They were baptized later in

the baptistry at Grafton Independent Baptist Church. (My

brother) Jim was baptized later at the same place."

From the beginning, the work was built on house-to-

house visitation, Bible preaching and teaching, and special

meetings. Our first step was door-to-door distribution of

flyers inviting residents to opening services. The twenty-two

people who met us on opening Sunday were the result of

this effort, or perhaps the ad placed in the Barbour

Democrat. Visitation generally consisted of follow-up visits to people who had visited the church as well as a continuation of door-to-door calling.

Hospital visits were made to people who had attended services or to people whose names were given me to visit. One time when I went into the hospital to visit, a nurse called me to see a patient who was very ill. I introduced myself as the pastor of New Testament Baptist Church, then gave him the gospel. When I asked him if he wanted to receive Christ, he said he did. He prayed to receive Christ, then I left him to rest and recover. On my next visit, he had recovered sufficiently to have gone home.

Carl Lanham took me to visit Mr. Stewart down Route 57. Carl had worked with him in the coal mines. I asked Mr. Stewart if he were saved. He said, "No." I asked him if I could tell him how to be saved. He said, "Yes." I explained how he could have his sins forgiven and become a child of God, then asked him if he wanted to be saved. He said, Yes, he did. I prayed with him as he invited Christ into his heart. Within a year he was in eternity. A daughter of his wrote to me and thanked me for witnessing to her dad and leading him to the Lord.

Some people were friendly, and I visited them frequently. Andy Compneal was one such person—always inviting me in, always ready to chat. Other people were indifferent, or downright hostile. I met one such person on the road to Arden. I drove into his driveway and walked up on his porch and knocked on his door. He opened the door, and I said, "I'm Allen Britt. I'm pastor of New Testament Baptist Church, and I'd like to . . . ."

At that point he said to me, "You get in your car and truck."

"What do you mean?" I asked, in my ignorance.

And he said, "You get out of here." In my great wisdom, I felt led to comply.

Our visits took us into homes of every kind--from the immaculate to the one that reeked of dog-aroma—and into situations of every kind. We found one of our young ladies up to her elbows in sausage on hog-killing day. In another home we helped churn butter in a jar. In another I inadvertently turned over a bottle of liquor under the sofa while the residents were telling me what good men they were.

At one home I came upon a birthday celebration for Grandpa Minor. Although I had missed eating the ramps (a strong-flavored wild onion native to West Virginia), I got to eat a generous serving of cake and ice cream with ramp-breath blowing my way.

Our son Andy always made himself at home—on either side of the tracks. Yet, in spite of his friendliness, he had some harrowing experiences. On one occasion we were visiting in a trailer on Chestnut Ridge when he was attacked by a dog. We were inside the trailer and heard him yell. All the adults rushed outside to find him holding the dog at

arm's length by the throat to keep him at bay. The owners

of the dog took over at that point and took the dog away to

tie him up.

On another occasion Andy was given a bicycle ride by

Barbie Roe while we were visiting her mom. Barbie brought

him back scraped from head to toe after a bicycle accident

in which she lost control of the bicycle.

Sometimes visits involved life-and-death situations.

On one occasion I was called to Mansfield to help a man

threatening suicide. When I got there, he had a kitchen

knife on the table in front of him. He told me he was going

to kill himself. I continued to talk to him until I talked him

out of it. When I got ready to leave, I asked him to give me

the knife. Although he refused, I felt confident that his crisis

had passed.

Another attempt to avert disaster was not so

successful. A Corley family with several young children had

been attending our church. The oldest child was a boy

Andy's age who came often or stayed after church to play

with Andy. The dad had been disabled in the Viet Nam War,

and they were waiting for his disability payments to begin.

We were all heart-broken when the wife took the

first disability check—and the children—and left for Ohio.

He was devastated. He refused our repeated attempts to

visit. He refused to come to church: she might call if he left

the house. In his despair he took his own life and left us

with heavy hearts.

Also tragic were the stories of those who lost their

opportunity to receive Christ. On one occasion Jennie and I

were knocking on doors in South Philippi when a relatively

young mother came to one door. When we offered to come

in and tell her how she could know for certain she was going

to Heaven when she died, she indicated that she would like

that. Then, almost as a second thought, she added, "Could

you come back in about an hour? My son is coming home from school, and I want him to hear this."

We were overjoyed at the prospect of pointing not just one, but two precious souls to Heaven. When we came back, however, the mother did not admit us, and we never had the opportunity to show her the Way.

The preaching ministry of New Testament Baptist consisted of a combination of topical, textual, and expository messages. Nearly always one series of expository messages was being preached on a Sunday night or a Wednesday evening. During the 12 years of ministry there I preached through Mark (1976), John (1977), I Corinthians (1979), Romans (1984), and Revelation. The longest-running series was a Wednesday night series on the Psalms— appropriate messages for a prayer meeting, since many of the psalms themselves are prayers. "The Blessings at the Bottom of the Barrel" was the longest-remembered textual message (I Kings 17). Perhaps it was because we experienced those blessings first-hand: money to buy shoes when we needed shoes; money to pay utilities when we needed to pay utilities; money to buy groceries when we needed groceries. Often we would go visiting and we would be given money to meet immediate needs. Other times the mail would bring much-needed funds.

One snowy winter day when Jennie was home with Andrew a man unknown to her walked up the outside stairs with a brown bag in his arms and knocked on the office door. Jennie answered the knock and heard the man say, "I'd like to give you this turkey."

"Why, thank you," she answered and accepted the brown bag, at the same time thinking, "What am I going to do with this turkey? It's almost Christmas, and we always go home for Christmas. They always have a turkey at home. I guess I'll just put it in the freezer for another time."

That "another time" came shortly after Christmas when friend Jeanne Ball called from Pennsylvania to ask if her son Jim and his family could stay with us on his way

south to look for work. When we learned that Jim was a

carpenter, my mind leaped to the work that needed to be

done on the building. We knew we couldn't pay him a

carpenter's salary, but he consented to work for a love

offering.

During the time Jim and his family were with us,

Jennie roasted the turkey. We ate roast turkey, turkey

sandwiches, turkey casseroles, turkey soup. The Lord knew

what we would need during those days that snow kept our

congregation home from church—and sent it in advance!

"The Blessings at the Bottom of the Barrel"

I Kings 17:1-16

I.   The Breakdown of Human Help

      A. Our Inability to save ourselves

      B. Our Failure to overcome sin habits

      C. Our Failure to solve life's problems

II.   The Bounty of God

A. God wants to meet all our need, large or

small. Jeremiah 33:3, Psalm 81:10

B. God meets all our needs through Christ,

our Lord. Philippians 4:13, 19

III. The Blessing of Giving

A. The widow discovered the joy of giving.

Acts 20:35

B. She discovered God's reward for sharing.

IV. The Bread of Life John 6:32-35, 47-51

A. God gave them bread to sustain life.

B. God gives us eternal life through Christ,

the bread of life.

Usually the children and adults met together for

worship services, but from the beginning the children met

separately for Sunday School. Until there were other

teachers, Jennie taught all the children in one class. Using

the Footsteps of Faith series published by Bible Club

Movement and supplementing it with original lessons, she

taught through the Bible from Genesis to Revelation.

On one bitterly cold Sunday in February the weather

kept the entire congregation away. When we thought there

would be just the three of us for Sunday School a new little

girl named Carla showed up just in time for Sunday School. I

had visited her family in an apartment over the Dollar Store

and invited them to church.

Jennie had prepared a special lesson for Valentine's

Day from the book of Jeremiah and illustrated it with

valentines. First, there was the called heart—Jeremiah's

heart, called to give God's message to God's people. Then,

there was the empty heart—Israel's heart, empty because

they had turned from the Lord and turned to vanities that

can never satisfy. Next was the broken heart—God's heart,

broken because His people had forsaken Him and forgotten

Him. Finally, there was the cleansed heart—the heart

cleansed through faith in the shed blood of Christ.

Carla listened attentively and indicated that she wanted to have a cleansed heart. She prayed, asking Christ to cleanse her heart and make her His child. When she came back the following Sunday, she amazed us all by reciting the last week's lesson nearly verbatim. She knew all about the called heart, the empty heart, the broken heart, and the cleansed heart.

Over the years the Lord sent us other teachers to minister to the children. Some of them were trained teachers, others we trained ourselves.

Chapter 15

TEACHING

As Andy approached school age, the question began to loom large in our minds, "What shall we do about his education?" Public education was not an option. The state could not teach our child the truths that God had commissioned us to teach him. The nearest Christian school was 25 miles away, a distance that we could not afford to drive every day.

While we mulled over this question, the Lord sent an answer in the form of a teen missions trip to Philippi from a church in Tennessee. The teens taught Bible clubs in the morning, worked on the building in the afternoon—scraping and painting the tall north wall of the building. Our days were busy shopping and preparing meals for the group. In the evenings we relaxed together in the cool waters of the Buckhannon River at Audra State Park.

During conversation at one mealtime we mentioned our dilemma. We had both taught older classes—third grade through high school—but had never taught kindergarten. We didn't know if we could do it. The teen sponsors told us about the A Beka curriculum. "It tells you what to do," they encouraged us. "It even tells you what to say."

"Well, we could do that," we thought, and soon we were making plans to begin Barbour Christian Academy. The church voted to start the Christian school as a ministry of New Testament Baptist Church. We conferred with a nearby pastor from Bridgeport who had experience in Christian School administration and with Dr. Phil Suiter, the president of the West Virginia Association of Christian Schools. At Dr. Suiter's advice, we went to the Barbour County School superintendent, told him what we planned to do, showed him the curriculum, told him we planned to be in session

180 days. He was supportive, offered us federal programs

that were available, and noted when we declined.

In September of 1979 the doors of Barbour Christian

Academy opened with one student and two teachers. The

following year a kindergarten student and two sisters,

kindergarten and first grade, joined us. Later the children of

Marvin Brown joined us (third grade through high school),

followed by Anna and William Gregory, then others from

more than a half dozen different families. Some came for

academic reasons, some for spiritual. We counted it a

privilege to minister to them all.

From the beginning we chose an eclectic

curriculum—for the most part A Beka for academics. For

elementary Bible we used Bible Guides A, B, and C from

Christian Schools International. All the elementary students

participated in the Bible story and Bible memory time. Then

the upper elementary students worked in their Bible

workbooks while the lower elementary students were

taught their next class: math. For high school Bible, the Bob

Jones curriculum was used: Old Testament Heroes and

Villains, the Life of Christ, Successful Christian Living.

Our schedule provided for a two-room school with

kindergarten through sixth grade in one classroom, seventh

through twelfth in another. While I taught Bible and history

to the high school students, Jennie taught phonics, reading,

and spelling to the elementary students. After morning

recess, I taught Bible and math to the elementary students

while Jennie taught English and math to the high school

students. In the last block of time—after afternoon recess—

I taught high school science while Jennie taught elementary

language and fine arts.

All our breaks were shared. Morning break was a

continuation of the physical education classes offered on

Monday at the Alderson-Broaddus auxiliary gym. Lunch in

the middle of the day we shared in the sun porch where the

high school classes met. Afternoon recess was free time,

with students playing basketball in the alley behind the

church, soccer or other games in the vacant lot behind the

church, jump rope, or hopscotch on our own small

playground.

The county provided us with the same testing

services they provided to the public schools. Our students

always performed well above the median, scoring within the

50th-60th percentile in math and science, above the 70th

percentile in language arts and social studies. One high

school student who came to us in need of remedial math

scored on 10th grade level after completing a 5th grade math

text!

The small size of our school enabled us to offer a

variety of activities to enrich the curriculum: the Monday

morning trip to the Alderson-Broaddus auxiliary gym for

physical education, occasional trips to the North Philippi

park to play tennis, field trips to pastors' fellowships as well

as to historic sites. The year we studied West Virginia

history, our field trips took us to the Indian mounds in

Moundsville; to Fort Ashby, one of the forts commissioned

by Colonel Washington on the frontier; to an operating grist

mill (closed for snow the day we were there); and to the

state Capitol.

Membership in the West Virginia Association of

Christian Schools enabled our students to participate in the

state academic, Bible, and fine arts competition. There our

students participated in a spelling bee, a recorder duet, and

a piano solo.

One of the highlights of each year was the field day

that climaxed our physical education program. Our program

emphasized physical fitness and used the presidential

physical fitness testing to challenge the students to excel.

Although they were competing against national standards,

their eyes saw only the other competitors. Those who made

the 50th percentile in any event were awarded ribbons at the

awards-day program at the end of the year.

Graduations were milestones for both the kindergarten and the high school graduates. The programs included dramas as diverse as "Little Bo Peep" (1987) and "Shelter from the Storm" (1988). Each program showcased academic skills—from Bible ABC's recited by kindergarten students to original research on West Virginia heroes by West Virginia history students.

Poetry, choral reading, and music highlighted the school's fine arts program. Music was chosen for its message as well as its musical impact, from the traditional:

"Jesu, Joy of Man's Desiring"	J. S. Bach
"Hallelujah, What a Savior"	P. P. Bliss
"Christ, the Lord is Risen Today"	Charles Wesley
to the new: "Mommie, You're Special"	Nicky Chavers

The song that made its way into our hearts and became a cherished memory of our West Virginia days was E. W. James' "My Home Among the Hills."

We were always grateful for the opportunity to educate our son in this unique setting. Although the academics kept us busy, our greatest thrill came in the first year of Barbour Christian Academy. One day a gentle reminder directed to son Andrew's misbehavior, "Andy, do you know that's why Jesus died—so he could pay for the bad things we do?" brought tears of repentance and a prayer to receive Christ as his Savior.

Chapter 16

REACHING

What the graduations and special programs were to the school, special meetings were to the church—an opportunity to advertise, an opportunity to minister to the community, an event to which our own people could look with anticipation and in which they could participate.

Some time after the Bennett Collins tent meeting and the Charles Hicks revival, I began thinking the time had come to organize as a church. Working from another church constitution as a model, we developed our own constitution, then made copies for each family then attending. I invited Al Dickerson as speaker and set a date for January of 1976. Those desiring to become members of New Testament Baptist Church signed the constitution as charter members and, at the suggestion of Pastor Dickerson, voted me as their pastor.

Some of the evangelists who came to Philippi we remembered for their visitation habits. John Winstead visited every day. He feared neither man or beast. He would walk right up to a barking dog and begin to pet it. Jeff Nichols also visited every day—whether I was able to go or not. He simply picked a street and knocked on every door. On one occasion we invited to Philippi Paul Rowden, who had a regular visitation ministry, going from one town to another, visiting on behalf of the host church. After two weeks of visiting in Philippi and preaching in the regular services, he told me frankly, "This is the coldest town I've ever been in."

Other evangelists were remembered for their personal habits. Wilda Lanham remembered serving a blueberry cheese cake to Dave Goodman and hearing his comment, "My idea of Heaven would be a giant cheese cake that would last forever." Wilda also remembered that Jim

Gent wouldn't eat dessert. We, too, remembered Jim as the

most disciplined in his personal habits of any of the

evangelists who stayed in our home. He came home from

the library one day after reading an article about caffeine

and told me, "You shouldn't drink that stuff (coffee). It's not

good for you."

I took his word for it and quit—cold turkey. The next

day I was so sick I couldn't go to church, so I told Jim,

"Brother Jim, you'll have to lead the singing."

"Oh, no problem," he replied, oblivious to the fact

that he couldn't carry a tune.

I could only guess what was happening downstairs

that night as I heard the piano start one song, then stop,

followed by another, then another stop. A sudden explosion

of laughter brought the song service to an abrupt end.

Only later did I learn what had happened. Jennie

would play an introduction to a congregational hymn, the

congregation would start to sing, then stop when Jim's fog-

horn monotone drowned everyone out. After two or three

false starts Jim quipped, "Well, I could sing if I had a pianist

who could play ...." That was the signal for all the pent-up

amusement to explode in the laughter I heard upstairs.

At least one evangelist was remembered for a single

message: Jerry Knight and his message "The Crimson

Worm." Based on the text, "I am a worm and no man . . ."

Psalm 22:6, the message identified Christ with the scarlet

worm used to dye scarlet. One visitor to that service said to

the lady who invited her, "I've been in church 70 years, and

that's the greatest sermon I've ever heard."

While we remembered Evangelist Knight for his

powerful message, we remembered others for their music:

Bennett Collins singing "Zion's Hill" and his wife's gifted

piano playing.

Yet, undoubtedly the most visible results came from

a meeting with Evangelist Don Williams shortly before

Christmas one winter. Crowds packed the house every night to hear him preach and to watch him illustrate his messages with chalk drawings.

While crowds listened to the messages and watched the drawing, and while visitors responded to the invitation to receive Christ, Jennie entertained the little ones in the nursery upstairs. She never forgot one little girl who responded every time she was asked if she were finished washing her hands, "Not 'et." We later learned that she did not have running water in her home. No doubt it was a luxury not to be readily relinquished.

Every year's schedule of special meetings included something special for the children. Leon and Brenda Foote and their son John used puppets to teach the children. Evangelist Irvy Hawkins used his ventriloquist dolls. Grace and Bob Claytor set up an elaborate ship and referred to themselves as Captain Bob and Shipmate Grace.

Other times we used talent closer to home to conduct our own Vacation Bible School. Carl and Dianne Doppel, from the church I had pastored in Oakland, came to help us with one VBS. We introduced them as Cowboy Carl and Princess Dianne. When I had to have emergency hernia surgery that week, Carl had to preach for me. On another occasion Harold Loucks and Jack Streets, neighboring pastors, provided skits to help us promote Vacation Bible School.

On several occasions our summer outreach to children took the form of 5-day clubs. The teens from Tennessee taught Bible clubs in several locations. A young man working with Child Evangelism Fellowship taught Bible clubs another summer. He taught us the song that became a favorite, "My God is So Big."

"My God is so big—so strong and so mighty—

There's nothing my God cannot do.

The mountains are His; the rivers are His.

The stars are His handiwork too." (Repeat Lines 1 &

2.)

One of the earliest Bible clubs—on the front porch of a

neighbor's house—gave us the opportunity to lead a dear

neighbor boy to Christ.

For a time we had an outreach ministry at the

Barbour County Jail. It had been initiated by Don Reynolds,

at that time a pastor in Huttonsville and a volunteer chaplain

at the Huttonsville Correctional Center. Every Thursday

night we would meet with the inmates for hymn singing and

Bible preaching. Later, a Mr. Velasquez, the father of one of

our Christian school students, joined us with his guitar. The

guitar was a big attraction to the inmates. Another big

attraction was the Bible study material published by Source

of Light Mission. For each completed lesson, the inmate

would receive a certificate.

One evening at the jail I was alone. The guards let

me in and locked me in the cell with the inmates. We all

gathered around the metal table in the center of the room

and sat on the metal chairs. After Bible study I looked for

the guards, who usually returned after an hour to unlock the

door and let me leave, but no guards came. For another

hour I talked with the prisoners and visited with them, all

the time wondering if I would have to spend the night there.

Finally, one of the prisoners was able to get the guard's

attention, and he came and let me out.

One year we participated in the Christmas parade as

an outreach ministry. Volunteers made the manger scene

and drove the truck that pulled the float. Our son Andy

dressed as a shepherd and rode on the float. We walked

beside the float distributing Christmas tracts along the way.

Because we had no baptistry of our own, baptisms

were always a special occasion, arranged in advance if we

were using another church's facilities, planned in advance if

we were using outdoor facilities. The very first baptism was

planned for Moatsville Junction. Here, in a sparkling pool

below the bridge, our dear Forrest Bartlett went under the waters of baptism, making public the faith he had claimed years before. At 88, he was the oldest person I had ever baptized. He was followed by Mary Reynolds and the five foster boys of the Clark family—Kevin and Lenny Skidmore, John, Jim, and L. J. Smouse.

The Grafton Church offered their facilities for the baptism of the Fridley family—Clayton, Flora, and Jim. Our son Andy and the Reynolds girls (Mary Reynolds' great-granddaughters) were baptized in the Calvary Baptist Church baptistry in Elkins.

On one occasion we baptized at a pond off 119 south of Philippi. The muck at the bottom of the pond prompted us to seek another location for another baptism. Pleasant Creek Wildlife Management Area provided that ideal outdoor location—a concrete ramp under our feet and the still waters of Tygart Lake before us.

We were headed to baptism there one summer Sunday afternoon of 1979 after the morning service. I was driving the 1972 Volkswagen we had bought new in Hagerstown, Maryland, after our older Volkswagen died on its way to my ordination in Elkton, Maryland, years before. The car was full.

Jennie's mom and dad were visiting, and Jennie was driving her dad's car to take home a handicapped lady who attended the morning service. As she headed north on 119 from Hacker Creek toward Pleasant Creek, she saw the Volkswagen sitting empty beside the road. "That looks like our car," she thought and continued to the baptism. After witnessing the baptism, she learned that it was indeed our car, that it had expired on the way to the baptism, and that we had been picked up by another vehicle heading to the baptism. Their eight passengers, added to our five from the Volkswagen, made a total of 13, possibly a record for a sedan!

Advertisement generally consisted of door-to-door distribution of flyers to advertise special meetings and advertisements in the <u>Barbour Democrat</u>. Occasionally special events would merit a write-up as an article in the local newspaper. Forrest Bartlett's birthday party merited such a write-up. Other articles featured school events: the poster contest—with pictures of the winning entries; academic, Bible, and fine arts competition; graduations. Yet, the most effective advertising was word-of-mouth advertising: neighbors telling neighbors, friends telling friends, family telling family.

Chapter 17

BUILDING

Six months after beginning services in May of 1975, the owner of the building declared bankruptcy, and the building was offered at public auction. Webb Butcher, the president of First National Bank, claimed the building as a foreclosure. I called Mr. Butcher to find out the status of the building and our status as renters. He told me that the bank, according to its by-laws, could not own property; that they would have to sell the building; and that we, as renters, had the first option to buy. He offered it to us for what was owed on the building--$16,000. We had to pay $2,000 down—due in one month from the date of his offer. We had no money in the church account. I had $5.00 in my pocket. But I said, "We'll take it."

Next Sunday I made known to our congregation what I had ventured. Within the month the entire amount—less $150—had been donated. Karen Brummett called me in Clarksburg on the day I was to meet Mr. Butcher and told me she'd meet me on the way to the bank. We met, and she gave me the $150 we needed to complete the down payment. For the ten years we paid on the building, we never missed a payment, and we never paid late. We made the down payment in December of 1975 and made the final payment in December of 1985.

Over the years we were constantly remodeling the building that was now ours. The Lord always supplied the money to buy materials and the men to do the work. Our first project was to remodel the upstairs and make it into an apartment for the pastor's family.

We chose a beautiful pecan paneling for the living room and the kitchen. The front sun room we partitioned to make a guest bedroom on one side and our bedroom on the other. My office, Andy's bedroom, and both bathrooms we painted. Jennie stripped and painted the old claw-foot tub in the big bathroom. The men installed a drop ceiling in the whole apartment. A brick-patterned linoleum covered the kitchen and living room floors, carpet Andy's bedroom, my office, and the small hall between. We were ready to move in the late summer of 1976.

The winter after our move found us in a very cold winter with very little heat. The former owner of the building had taken the heating units when he lost the property. We had only a small space heater to heat the entire upstairs. Jennie remembered sitting in front of the space heater to read. Her front would be warm, but her back would be cold. In spite of our concern for Andy, he was always warm when we stopped what we were doing to see if he was okay. Jennie did a lot of baking to keep the kitchen warm. Eventually we were able to purchase a furnace and have it installed with duct work to heat the upstairs.

Early in our occupation of the building Jennie's mom and dad discovered that we had beautiful hardwood floors and undertook to refinish them. We rented an electric sander to remove the old finish. They applied polyurethane for the new finish. Some time later Jennie and I undertook to refinish the pine floor in the front sun room. First, we had to remove the old tile—scraping away not only the tile, but also the tar paper underneath. Then the sander took the floor to the bare wood, so that we could apply polyurethane for the finish. We learned that pine is a soft wood, easy to gouge with a sander, but still attractive when finished.

When we bought the building, we inherited a very old porch and a very steep set of stairs on the south side of the building. We probably did not realize how steep those stairs were until my mother-in-law came to visit and climbed them on her hands and feet! Yet, we did not do anything about the steps until one of the men—Jim Clark—suggested that we insulate and shingle the building on the south and

east sides. Now the porch had to go!

One Saturday—Labor Day weekend of 1977—the

men from the church gathered with their tools in hand to

disconnect the old porch and send it crashing to its demise.

Our little pre-schooler, Andy, always in the middle of the

action, decided to dart across the yard at the very moment

the porch came down and narrowly escaped serious injury.

The next project—insulating and shingling the

building—became a long, drawn-out process. We started on

the east end—the front facing Walnut Street. Jim Clark was

the first to work on the project. My father-in-law, when he

came to visit, worked on the insulation on the south side.

Jennie and I would hold the sheathing from the top of the

building while he nailed it in place from a ladder.

Missionaries Larry Parshall and Charles Deaton were among

the visiting missionaries who worked on the project. The

final shingles were nailed in place by a local man who

volunteered to finish the project.

Eventually we replaced the old steps with a new set,

sturdy and safer, with a much less steep incline, from the

side entrance nearest the street to the upstairs office door.

A visiting cat once sat on these steps as the Sunday morning

service began. One of the ladies felt that it was not a good

testimonial to our singing ability when the cat got up and

walked away as the song service began.

The tall north wall of the building needed to be

scraped and painted. The Tennessee teens who came to

help us one summer undertook this project. They

assembled the scaffolding we had rented, and scraped and

painted through a week of long summer afternoons. In the

evenings we took them to the Buckhannon River at Audra

State Park to relax and refresh in the cool waters.

Jennie finished the renovation of the building by

staining the back porch the summer of my brother Tom's

visit. We were thinking the back porch would make a good place for the kids to play if it rained during their visit. No rain came, but the back porch served as a picnic shelter for a later birthday party. It also provided a place to hang laundry to dry outdoors.

Even before the renovation of the building was complete, I was thinking of widening the sanctuary. We were meeting in a long, narrow room on one side of the building partitioned from two smaller Sunday School rooms on the other side. I wanted to take out the partition and double the space for our sanctuary.

One cold January day a call from Hartstown, Pennsylvania, made this desire into a possibility. Our friend Jeanne Ball was calling to tell us that her son Jim was on his way south to look for work. Would we give Jim and his family a place to stay on their way south? Of course—we had been friends of the Ball family since we were their neighbors in Chattanooga and fellow students at Tennessee Temple.

When we learned that Jim was a carpenter, we told him what we'd like to do to the sanctuary and asked if he'd be willing to work on the project for a love offering. We knew we couldn't pay him carpenter's wages! He was willing, and so the project was underway.

Jim told me we would need a beam to support the upstairs when we took out the support wall. We borrowed a truck from Shorty Stalnaker and drove to a lumber yard in Belington. After telling us it couldn't be done, the man at the lumber yard lifted the beam (8"x 12" x20') on a fork lift and placed it in the bed of the truck. The beam extended beyond the bed of the truck and hung just inches above the road. The lumber yard man flagged it for us and sent us on our way.

When we got to the church, we backed the truck up to the door and slid the beam onto steel pipes that we used as rollers. After Jim took the wall down, we used a scaffold

that he had built to inch the beam up into place. Steel posts

supported the beam. From the local builders' supply we

bought paneling. Not only did Jim panel the new sanctuary,

he also boxed in the steel posts with paneling. When we

later added carpet, our new sanctuary was complete.

Now we felt we could settle into a routine of

ministry. School hours, Monday through Friday, we spent in

the classrooms. After school we snatched an hour for rest

and recuperation before commencing afternoon duties.

Jennie went to the kitchen to get supper; I went to the office

to prepare the next message; Andy went outside to play or

to practice seasonal sports: baseball in spring, soccer in the

fall, basketball in winter. After supper Andy practiced piano

while Mom washed dishes. Then we studied with Andy

whatever lessons he needed to prepare, read the Bible and a

Keys for Kids story with him and tucked him into bed. After

he was tucked into bed, we went downstairs to prepare for

the next day's classes.

Chapter 18

SHUT IN

It was while preparing the board work for the next day's lessons one Monday evening in November of 1985 that we became aware that a flood was on its way. Firemen in the street were evacuating residents of our block, the block nearest the flooding Tygart River. Because we lived upstairs in the building, it was considered safe for us to stay.

When an older lady across the street refused to leave her home, we offered our place as a shelter. She was willing to stay with us, since we were close to her home. When the firemen brought her to our door, we ushered her upstairs to the care of Geraldine Semmelman, our permanent house guest. Geraldine made a bed for her on the sofa, while we went back downstairs to prepare our own building for the anticipated flood.

At that point our vision of the coming flood was based on stories we had heard residents tell of previous floods: basements flooded, first-floor carpets damaged. We could envision water covering the floor and the lowest shelves of the book cases. Our priority at that point was to take to safe-keeping the expensive A Beka curriculum guides we used for the lower elementary grades. These Andy and I, dressed in our boots, carried to the stairway and handed to Jennie, who hauled them upstairs to store on a table in the laundry room. Next, we carried the students' books from the storage spaces under their desks. By now the water that we had heard swirling under the building was rising into the building. We continued working, sloshing through the rising waters, until we had emptied the bottom shelves of the book cases, stacking the books on the teachers' desks.

Jennie's last act before retreating upstairs was to take the bottom drawer out of the filing cabinet and put it on top of the filing cabinet. There, her music and the new

Hymnplayer books she had bought for Andy were safe. She thought.

Although we did go to bed—and to sleep—we awakened often during the night, going to the window each time to see how much the water had risen and going to the back door to gauge the water level by the garage below. By morning the water had risen to the top of the garage window. And by morning only the top of Andy's gym set was visible—protruding through the branches of the giant maple in the side yard. Only when the waters receded would we know that his gym set had been entirely uprooted—cement footers and all—and wrapped around that tree!

During the night we could hear the furniture bumping together in the sanctuary below. We assumed those sturdy wooden pews would survive. We would only need to hose them off when this was over. We assumed the piano was safe. We had moved it to the speaker's platform before we left to come upstairs.

By day we realized we were no longer a block away from the Tygart River. We were in the middle of it! The rushing waters that isolated us in our upstairs "island" also carried along with it the accumulated debris from other flooded buildings in its path. From our windows we watched floating packages of sausages from the corner Foodland float by. Smiling faces of Charmin children greeted us as they floated by. A giant red box—that we later learned was a Coke machine—bobbed in the back yard of our neighbor's house.

Against all warnings: "The waters are polluted. Do not attempt to salvage or eat anything from the flood waters," neighbor teens carried on a salvage operation from their own flooded back yard. One teen, precariously perched on a fallen tree, snared and tossed to another teen at the second story window above him, giant packages of potato chips and whatever else came within reach.

We were now without electricity and subsequently, without heat. With five mouths to feed, Jennie improvised by holding a soup can with a pair of tongs over a candle flame until it was somewhat warm. We learned later that we fared better than one neighbor who stayed upstairs in her house and ate only a package of mints the day of the flood. The weather was mild; we did not suffer from the cold.

It was the next day—after the flood waters had receded—before we could leave our "island" and assess the damage. Jennie found that, even with her boots on, the steps to the downstairs were treacherous with mud. Every step required an effort to keep from sliding. She ventured far enough to see, however, that the water level was just above the file drawer she had placed on top of the filing cabinet. Its contents were just as wet and muddy as they would have been had they been left in place!

Beyond that middle room, the utter chaos of the sanctuary, with benches piled on top of benches, discouraged any further exploration. From the outside of the building, however, we could see that the piano we had assumed safe was no longer in its place. It was lying on its back in one corner of the sanctuary.

And what a shambles did we find outside the building! The garage that we had used to gauge the level of the rising water no longer existed! Only a portion of the north wall remained standing. The cement blocks from the west wall lay strewn about the alley behind us. The window that had marked the level of the water as the flood crested, now dangled from an unsupported roof. The entire south wall was gone. Although we had read about floods before—the Johnstown Flood, in particular—nothing that we had read adequately conveyed two of the flood's most destructive features: 1-) the immense volume of mud moved by the flood, not from the bed of the river only, but also from all the ground traversed in its path, and 2-) the awesome power of the water as it moves at incredible speeds, moving everything movable in its path and, in turn, hurling those objects against the immovable objects in its path like a battering ram.

All the missiles picked up by the flood in its headlong plunge of destruction had been hurled against the back of the building as by a battering ram. Among those objects, a car still littered the alley. Other neighbors had souvenirs from the local funeral home and the local tire shop: tires in abundance and coffins littered the neighborhood.

As we surveyed the damage, others, too, were wandering the streets—some in a kind of daze, not yet comprehending the loss that had been incurred nor the massive clean-up that still lay ahead. As we compared notes, something amazing occurred on that day. A sense of camaraderie was born that had never before existed

between us "outsiders" and the "old-timers" of Philippi. We

had lived through "the Flood of the Century." Together we

had survived. And that survival had won our acceptance

into their number.

Clean-up began in earnest on the second day after

the flood when a work crew arrived from the Grafton

Independent Baptist Church. They helped us remove

furniture from the building and shampoo the newly-installed

carpet. The contents of the filing cabinet were piled onto

the growing mountain of debris at the back of the lot.

Jennie cried for the only time in the aftermath of the flood

when she saw the new Hymnplayer books on top of the

debris.

Now it was time for the tedious task of cleaning the

contents of the building. The filing cabinet itself, empty of

its contents, was scrubbed inside and out. Toothbrushes

brushed the mud from the grooves on which the rollers ran.

Jennie's canned goods from the pantry downstairs were washed in bleach water. The seals had not been broken; they would be good for another winter's fare.

The desks and bookshelves from the school rooms, the pulpit from the sanctuary—all could be scrubbed and salvaged. All the paper products had to go: hymn books and visualized songs for the children, Jennie's personal collection of hymn books, charts and flashcards for the school. Although we grieved the loss of handmade visuals, we did not attempt to replace them with handmade. When the time came to replace them, we ordered from our curriculum supplier.

While we worked downstairs, a faithful member of the crew worked upstairs to keep water boiling on the stove. Geraldine Semmelman was our indispensable water-purifier. When we emptied one bucket of muddy water, she had freshly-boiled water waiting for us to start again. When we were ready to collapse at the end of the day, she had boiled enough water to heat our baths. Water for cooking, water

for dish-washing—she boiled it all so that we had purified

water for every need.

While we were working on the contents of the

building, the piano and pews were drying in the front yard.

The pews we had hoped to salvage split into narrow slices of

wood as they dried in the sun. To the rubbish heap they

must go. When the piano had completely dried, not one key

could be pressed: dried mud filled every crevice between

the keys. It, too, must be relegated to the rubbish heap.

In the midst of these discouraging days, helpers

appeared from many directions. From the south, Downing

Gregory offered to clean the gas pipes so that our heat could

be restored. From the west, Pastor Bill Hawkins offered the

use of his church building, a former two-room school, for the

relocation of our school. From the hill above us, an official

of Alderson-Broaddus College offered us a meeting room for

Sunday morning services.

During the week following the flood, all schools were closed. We were working, as were other local residents, to clear the debris. City waste management crews hauled away trash by the truckload. City officials visited homes and businesses in the flood zone to determine if each was safe for occupation. The house behind our building was condemned: it had moved off its foundation. Another house across the street was condemned.

We had not yet formulated plans for repair when our building was visited by the city officials: the fire marshall, the health official, the building inspector. They informed us that our building would have to be repaired according to their specifications before it would be approved for occupancy. The carpet would have to go: it was polluted from the flood waters. The old insulation would have to be replaced. The walls and ceiling would have to be replaced with 5/8" sheetrock to provide a fire barrier between upstairs and downstairs and between the furnace and the meeting-rooms. A fire alarm system would have to be installed for the safety of the children who met there for school.

The first step in repairing the flood damage was to remove the soggy insulation behind the walls. Paneling had to be removed, the insulation scooped into buckets and dumped onto the growing mountain of debris. Front-end loaders from the city maintenance department loaded the debris into trucks to be hauled away.

Our next step in the repair process was to replace the blow-in insulation with rolls of fiberglass insulation. A work crew from southern West Virginia framed the meeting room for the new sheet rock. A local electrician donated his time to install the fire alarm system. Volunteers installed the new sheet rock. Only the carpet was installed professionally—by the people from whom we bought the carpet.

As re-opening day approached, we were scouting the "For Sale" section of the local newspaper for a used piano in good condition. After one disappointing trip to Elkins to consider a Baldwin unworthy of the name, we had decided on a rebuilt Knabe recommended by our friend Blaine Corder. When we asked the seller to delay delivery until the carpet could be installed, however, they canceled our order instead. Another "For Sale" search led us to a studio upright in good condition that became our church instrument and our personal piano as well.

AFTERWORD

(Note: The previous account marks the end of Allen's recorded memories, recorded just days before his first stroke September 10, 2010.)

Although the flood was not the end of the ministry in Philippi, it definitely was a turning point. For one thing, the ministry no longer seemed tied to a place. Visitors joined us for services on the Alderson-Broaddus campus who had not joined us on Walnut Street. Meeting in homes for prayer meetings allowed us to minister to people to whom we could not minister on Walnut Street. And the relocation of the school to the Volga location gave the students memories of a delightful school year. Those memories culminated in the first Barbour Christian Academy high school graduation to a packed house at Bethel Independent Baptist Church, the host church which allowed us to use their building after the

flood.

As another indication of this turning point, we began

to consider the possibility that the ministry might be ready

for new leadership. In consideration of this possibility, we

accepted an invitation to visit a church in Williamsport,

Pennsylvania, looking for teachers for their Christian school.

We liked the location. Williamsport, we felt, was a beautiful

city. We felt comfortable, too, with the church. We had

known friends from the church during our days at Temple.

But this was not God's open door for us. We could not find

a place to live. Neither did we find the peace to assure us of

God's direction. We were only days away from the beginning

of a new school year. How could we tell the parents of our

school students at this late date that we would not be

continuing the Christian school? We could not. We came

back to Philippi convinced that God would have us continue.

And continue we did. The following year saw new visitors in the church—many, students from Alderson-Broaddus College. And, a quite successful school year brought us to our second high school graduation, the first in our own building. Three kindergarten students graduated with our one high school senior. Kindergartners starred in a musical dramatization of "Little Bo Peep." High schoolers read original research from their West Virginia history class.

The following year the thought continued to persist that the time had come for the ministry to benefit from new leadership. This thought prompted us to invite a missionary of our acquaintance who was coming home from a short-term missionary assignment to visit us in Philippi and consider taking the ministry. He did visit, but did not feel that Philippi was God's direction for him. He did, however, make a recommendation that we felt led to follow: that we contact mission boards that might be willing to continue the ministry by placing a missionary there. One mission board was not interested: Philippi, they felt, did not have enough

population to offer the possibility of developing into a self-

supporting church. The second contact—to a missionary we

knew personally—brought a positive response. Allen had

preached several times for Pastor Gail Cutlip in Marlinton,

West Virginia. After a time of directing the mission board,

Brother Cutlip now wanted to get back into the ministry. He

himself would like to take the work!

We were elated when the church voted to call him as

pastor. Here was a man who truly loved the Lord, who loved

people, who was himself a native West Virginian, and who

had proved himself to have the stick-to-it-iveness required

of a missionary church planter in West Virginia.

Meanwhile, God had opened a door of service for us

to a Christian school ministry in Virginia. Brother Dave

Nicklas, our A Beka Book representative in West Virginia,

had accepted a position as principal of Grace Baptist School

in Petersburg, Virginia. He needed teachers and invited us

to come consider teaching positions. We felt an immediate

kinship with Pastor Nunnally and a quiet assurance that this

was God's direction for our lives. It would be a ministry of

teaching for us both, of visitation for Allen, and, for Allen

also, of preaching in three nursing home ministries:

Thursday evenings at Walnut Hill Convalescent Center,

Sunday afternoons at Mayfair House, and Friday evenings

(once a month) in Colonial Heights.

Days of preparation for the move to Petersburg were

busy days: sorting, packing, selling accumulated items no

longer needed in an end-of-mission porch sale, giving away

my childhood doll collection with the realization that I would

never have the money to refurbish their aging bodies. On

moving day we bought a new refrigerator, delivered and

loaded in its box, so that we could leave the matching stove

and refrigerator in the kitchen for the new pastor.

We looked forward with anticipation to the

opportunities that lay ahead. For Andy, there would be a

wider circle of friends in a larger Christian school. There

would be more opportunities for athletic participation:

softball on the church softball team, basketball on the high

school team, soccer on a community team. There would be

new opportunities for ministry for him: singing in church

services, preaching in a local mission. Yet, we knew, even in

view of the opportunities that lay ahead, that West Virginia

would always occupy a huge portion of our hearts. We

knew, even as we headed from the mountains to the Fall

Line of the Piedmont, that we would come back often—as

often as opportunity allowed-- to visit the people and the

land we loved.